CW00530259

Taking the Macho Out of Management

PADDY O'BRIEN is a personnel training consultant. She has been increasingly interested in observing the development of innovative management styles over the last few years, and has gathered her thoughts together in this thought-provoking new book. Paddy is a black-belt martial artist and a yoga teacher, and her understanding of the use of power in these disciplines brings fresh insights into the field of power management. Paddy lives in Berkshire with her partner and five children.

Sheldon Business Books

Sheldon Business Books is a list which exists to promote and facilitate the adoption of humane values and equal opportunities integrated with the technical and commercial expertise essential for successful business practice. Both practical and theoretical issues which challenge today's workforce will be explored in jargon-free, soundly researched books.

The first titles in the series are:
Taking the Macho Out of Management
by Paddy O'Brien
How to Succeed in Psychometric Tests by David Cohen
Making Change Work for You
by Alison Hardingham

Paddy O'Brien **Taking the Macho Out of Management**

Sheldon Business Books

sheldon^{PRESS}

First published in Great Britain 1993
Sheldon Press, SPCK, Marylebone Road, London NW1 4DU

© Paddy O'Brien 1993

British Library Cataloguing-in-Publication Data
A catalogue record for this book is available from the British
Library
ISBN 0-85969-656-1

Typography by Daniel Edwards
Photoset by Deltatype Ltd, Ellesmere Port, Cheshire
Printed in Great Britain at the University Press, Cambridge

To Tim

Contents

Acknowledgements and Dramatis Personae

I'd like to acknowledge insights and anecdotes shared by many, many delegates on courses I have run, and many conversations with colleagues at Quality and Equality of Oxford, and the Independent School for Conflict Management in Berkshire. Joan Orme and Julia Pokora are always sources of expert and sharp perception. In addition to this I had detailed interviews with the following people who contributed a wealth of thinking and experience:

Simon Ayres is forty-one and is an Area Manager in Social Services.

David Britton is forty-five and is European Finance Director of an international chemicals company.

Siobhan Boyle is forty-three and is Women's Officer in a Local Authority in the Midlands.

Derek Crispin is thirty-seven and is an Independent Financial Consultant.

Phoebe Driscoll is thirty-eight and is Operations Manager in a nationwide employment agency.

Mark Ellis is forty-nine and is headmaster of a Community school.

Cara Frances is thirty-eight and is Senior Editor in a multinational publishing corporation.

Neil Glover is forty-three and is a training consultant working in schools and voluntary organizations. He has been both a headmaster and director of an inner city community centre.

Michael Groves is thirty-nine and is Field Director of an Archaeological Trust.

Chris Hargreaves is forty-two and is Director of Housing in a London Borough.

Janet King is thirty-five and is Deputy Director of Education and Leisure Services in a London Borough.

Sean McCann is thirty-eight and is a partner in a firm of chartered accountants.

Dr Paul Norton is forty-three and is Lecturer in a University English Department.

Julia Primera is thirty-eight and has worked in a multinational oil company. She is now a management consultant.

Leonard Rawlins is thirty-five. He has worked for several national charities. He is now an O.D. consultant in the Voluntary Sector.

Samantha Rossiter is thirty-nine. She is an administrative officer.

Parminder Sharma is thirty-six. She is Corporate Development Officer in a national broadcasting organization.

Angela Winters is thirty-two. She is Senior Research Executive in a Qualitative Market Research organization.

Joan Yates is forty. She is Senior Lecturer in Social Work Studies in a university.

These people come from private sector, public sector, voluntary sector, and educational roles, and bring special material from each. These are not their real names, but they know who they are, and I thank them very much. I also want to thank Tim for many useful discussions.

Paddy O'Brien, October 1992

Introduction

This is a book for anyone who has moved recently into the management tier and wants to think through their style, their development and their leadership qualities, and also for anyone who has been a manager for some time and wants to review alternative styles and refresh their energies.

It grows from the observation that the 1980s was a period of ruthless opportunistic growth combined with a significant shift in assumptions about social responsibility. For the first time significant numbers of women were making headway into the professions and the managerial ranks, despite the notorious glass ceiling; but their arrival did not bring the dawn of a softer management style. In fact rather the reverse happened, with women achieving more or less in proportion to their ability to act like men. The advertising industry spawned the twin icons of the gelled, fast, brash executive man, and the shoulder-padded shortskirted 'executive tart', as frightening a pair of role models, in retrospect, as you could hope to find.

Talk was of 'in the real world' and 'the bottom line' and making huge amounts of speculative money was thought of as clever, where, with an ever-rising stock market it was simply inevitable.

I joined this culture as much as I could and as much as it would let me, and ran around trying to look important like everybody else. However, for me as for everybody else the nineties have come and 'real life' now consists of multiple recessions and people in city centres leading more or less feral lives in cardboard boxes.

In the 1980s it was fashionable and smart to be ruthless and thrusting. Times have changed. The growth curve was not self-sustaining. Now we need a management style which can respond to the ups and the downs, the successes and the crashes, the ebbs and flows of the nineties. Every manager has to maximize profits. The myth that this necessitates behaviour destructive to self and others has been exploded. The aim now is to create a workplace both realistic and humane for the future.

I began to see how this might be possible during a martial arts grading when I had to break a pile of roof tiles with a knife hand strike. I prepared the same way everybody does for that test by going through the motions of the strike over and over again: but you are not allowed to practise beforehand. If you have learned your strike correctly, it will work, if you have not it will not – simple as that.

I did no positive thinking whatsoever: in fact I was convinced I could not do it. I walked out into the centre of the hall feeling fatalistic. I got into the correct position, steadied my breathing, and that strange auditory exclusion happened that comes when you are really concentrating. People were wandering in and out, talking, training in other parts of the hall, but I couldn't hear them at all. I did the strike correctly. The tiles broke. I felt full of relief and elation. It is no big deal, everyone who takes that test in that style has to do the same thing, but it meant a lot to me.

Doing the strike, I learned something very strange: and it took root in my mind because it linked up with so many other perceptions I was having while working in management training. I realised that my hand did not go through the tiles because I hit them hard – I could sense that if I had done that I would simply have hurt my hand. It went through because I hit them *gently*. I thought of the tension and aggravation experienced by people in management positions as they tried to cope with office politics, ride the recession, and get their staff to perform. I had a sense that a lot of energy gets wasted that way, and a lot of damage done. I had a powerful sense of the unstoppability of focused, clear, *gentleness*.

This is an exploratory book rather than a 'how to' book. In it you will hear the considerations of managers in the public, private, and voluntary sectors, when they start to talk and think about the issue of 'macho' behaviour and their own and their colleagues' management style. You will also find some 'triggers' to help prompt in your own mind some querying and thinking about your own way of working. Perhaps a useful place to start would be to recall any times in your own life, when suddenly, unexpectedly, you prevailed, even though you expected to fail. See if you can work out what the key to that success was, and bear it in mind as you begin to read.

Note: Needless to say, it is not a good idea to verify this by going out into the garden and starting to hit tiles; that particular skill is part of specialised training. It is the principle that is important.

1. Whatever happened to leading from the front?

For a long time, the fantasy of tough leadership has informed our concept of what a manager should be. Macho management is exhausting for men and incongruous for women but nevertheless women and men struggle daily to fit themselves into that mould because we think that is what will give us credibility in the management tier. It is by no means always the best use of our energies, however, and we will be investigating the mix of qualities and styles which would give us a maximum return and an optimum range.

Behaviour in the workplace has to be re-negotiated all the time. We need to re-negotiate in the light of Equal Opportunities legislation, in the light of new Quality procedures, in the light of recession or boom, European directives, awareness of sexual harassment, integrating new technologies, and a hundred other issues. Reviewing and re-thinking our management style is rewarding because it helps us to meet all these challenges more effectively. It is rewarding because it gives us clues how to drive our energies well without burning out; and finally it is rewarding because it gives us a time to reflect not only on the push for success, but also on exactly what our own personal sense of satisfaction and fulfilment comes from, so that, in the rush of a busy life, we do not wake up one day and find we have lost touch with it.

In fact there are probably times in most management jobs where it is appropriate and necessary to be macho, if by macho we mean abrupt, directive and uncompromising. This book is not about how never to be macho again. It is about realizing that there are a great many other notes in the managerial scale than just machismo, and that a range and mixture of them will probably be a great deal more effective and enjoyable than a machismo monotone.

Why does it matter to us what sort of managers we have? Why does it matter to us what sort of managers we are? It matters because we are aware at both an intellectual and a gut level that the quality of management we get and the quality of management we give is a crucial determinant of the quality of work and performance that results. Shaping raw energy into productive effort, turning good ideas into effective action, keeping an organization in-budget, up-to-date, and developing, all come from good management. Idea-to-action rests on good management, and staff development does too. Making sure the right training happens at the right time, so that staff have the opportunity to reach their full potential, rests on good management. Good counselling and flexible planning can ensure that illness or personal difficulties do not wreck careers or disrupt productivity. Crises and personality clashes arise in any workplace. Whether they lead to disaster or get resolved into new opportunity depends on how they are managed.

Thus we have a very close interest in how we are managed and how we are managing. We can, in the main, assume that our work is good and our ideas constructive, and those of our staff likewise, but we know how much, how very much, depends on how those qualities and efforts are channelled.

Let us look at the rich mix of qualities which come into good leadership. When you become a leader, you bring baggage of good and bad kinds evolved from your own experiences of having been led. It is valuable to become aware of this baggage and to assess it, so that you can actively choose how much to imitate what you have experienced yourself, and avoid replicating behaviour that you found unhelpful and negative in people who have managed you.

TRIGGER ONE:

Ask yourself – what is the best leadership I have ever experienced? What were the qualities and style of that leadership, and what effect did it have on me?

Leaders in youth or childhood

Leadership does not only happen at work. It can be invaluable to notice when you have been well led in other parts of your life, and to reflect on what the qualities of that leadership were that made it special. They may well be transferable to your own style or your own situation at work. Even if they are not, you may be able to work out how that good leadership made you *feel*, and therefore how your staff might like to feel; and then you can work out how to help them feel it!

For example, Samantha Rossiter, a 39-year-old administrative officer, says:

> When I think about good leaders the person who comes into my mind is the man who was my teacher in the fourth year of the junior school. There were forty-four of us in the class and yet we were all always doing hard work at exactly the right level for us as individuals. We did maths, English and projects, and the room was always busy and concentrated with a kind of slight hum of activity. Although the day was structured and discipline was very firm, he sometimes used to let himself and us run with an idea, for a half day or a whole day if we all felt like it. At the time I took him completely for granted, but I think I have never since felt my own abilities so clearly perceived and drawn out, nor felt, in a sense, so safe in a very structured day which nevertheless had space for inspiration and creativity when it caught alight.
>
> Thinking about him now, I suppose what I would like to transfer to my own situation is to get to know my staff very, very well as individuals and to be pushing them all the time so they never get bored and always achieve that little bit more than they thought they could. I realize too that he must have done an extraordinary amount of planning. Since there were five or six different levels of activity going on at any one time, he must have been in effect preparing five or six different lessons each time. I think *very* good preparation has got to be the key to what I want to transfer – so that people feel completely secure that you know what you're doing, that everything's in hand.

The teaching that Samantha experienced happened more than twenty-five years ago. Teaching, since, has gone through arguably the two most difficult decades of its existence as a profession. Low pay, low morale and constant bureaucratic interference have undermined the efforts of those still courageous enough to involve themselves in it. However, we should remember what exceedingly powerful people teachers are, spending many hours per day directing the activities and being the role models for young people at the most impressionable time of their lives. If as a country we cannot any longer bring ourselves to invest in education for humane reasons – for the good of the children and the growth of knowledge – we should think very seriously indeed about doing so for business reasons. Leadership skills so badly needed in industry and commerce now may well not be in place because the young people entering the workforce were *not* taught by vigorous, competent, skilled teachers at school.

David Britton is forty-five years old and is European Finance Director of a large multinational chemical company. In spite of his extensive worldwide business experience, the best leadership he has encountered was as a very young man in a high level football team. Aged eighteen, he was a few years younger than the rest of the team, and says:

> The age difference felt big at the time. What I valued was the fact that the captain took time to talk me through every game, and gave me lots of praise.

Having his game attended to and developed at a young age has stayed in David's mind as a powerful example of good leadership, and that good attention and developmental discussion is certainly something we need to carry forward as an important strand in our leadership style.

Charismatic example

Looking back over the leadership they have received, many of today's managers remember a charismatic or inspirational figure who was outstanding in their lives.

Dr Paul Norton is a lecturer at a university who in common with many academics these days has a managerial as well as a technical role. He remembers a charismatic figure who affected his views on leadership and motivation.

> Between the ages of about seventeen and twenty I was very involved in the CND, the Quaker movement, and the Labour Party. A group of us, all about that age, with those commitments, grouped ourselves around one young man. He was very definitely a leader, and it was wonderful leadership, led by conviction. He was well-organized and thoughtful and planned ahead, I see that now. He was very sexual, political and charismatic. He was a focus for that group and made it a good place to be, although I think the young women found it harder to find their place and tended to take a subordinate role.

The sense of vision of this young man made him special, and the fact that that vision was backed up by good organisation turned him into an exceptional 'leader' to this informal but highly active and cohesive team. It is interesting that Paul chooses the word 'sexual' to describe him: there certainly is an area where the focused energy of a good leader makes them 'attractive' in a general sense (the team likes that leader, prefers to stay with her or him) which is very similar to being 'attractive' in a sexual sense – that is, where a certain vibrancy and radiance is specifically personally attractive. Most people whose energies are flowing well give out a kind of physical magnetism, regardless of their age or looks.

Neil Glover, who at forty-three has run both schools and community centres and now acts as a consultant to a wide range of voluntary and public sector organizations, also identifies his best leaders as having 'an explicit emotional commitment to an ideology'. He goes on:

> I was in my mid-twenties which is make or break time for teachers, and I was lucky enough to work for a headmaster who made no bones about his emotional commitment. The setting of a moral character was directly translated into actions and decisions. He was touched with a kind of naivety and

innocence. I'm still looking for that firm moral base in myself, but can't always translate that straight into action.

A charismatic leader can remain in the mind as a touchstone to check with for decades afterwards: as Nigel says: 'I still do things and think – "yes, that's OK, Tim would have done that" '.

Angela Winters is a senior research executive in qualitative market research at thirty-two years of age. For her, the dynamic of this type of leadership is a *sine qua non*. She says:

> Without charismatic leadership I would change jobs. My Managing Director, who is female, is young, dynamic, and has infectious enthusiasm and a keen sense of humour. She is considered to be 'tough for a woman', but I find that a derogatory comment which doesn't fit at all. She's just got a firm conviction about what needs doing and is able to communicate it. I'm very organized, so I can cope with the pragmatic side of work with ease. I prefer plenty of emotional inspiration.

Thus, Angela identifies her need for style of leadership which fills in the qualities she feels she has less of herself.

In addition to giving a crucial injection of positive energy, charismatic leaders may exemplify a particular style. At a critical point in his career Derek Crispin found an important leadership figure for him was 'a retired army officer who is immaculately well-organized, highly intelligent, and very self-disciplined', a standard Derek still finds himself trying to live up to.

Excellent professional practice combined with an exciting personality generated a model of leadership which Michael Groves, a thirty-nine-year-old field director in Archaeology, finds important. Like Neil, he often hears the echo of a previous and much-admired boss saying, for example, 'If you only *need* to do it once, don't do it twice', and even more basic maxims like 'Never make a wasted journey' (i.e. always carry something with you that needs to go to the same destination you are heading for). This man could, says Michael, 'Motivate staff to perform a high quality of work in impossible and even dangerous circumstances, by leading by example'.

In some areas one sometimes finds a leader who is exceptionally charismatic. It is a life-changing occurrence when one does: reflect on whether this has happened to you, and how it has affected you if it has.

I have come across this type of leadership twice – once directly and once indirectly, and both in the world of physical expression. Mr Iyengar is a teacher of yoga who has inspired students and teachers of yoga all over the world for fifty years. Many people, including myself, have found his work controversial, and have sometimes profoundly disagreed with his point of view. The slavish discipleship of some of his followers has sometimes seemed disturbing. I have never been to a class of his, either in his ashram in Pune, or when he has taught in the UK on his world tours. Yet through his books, through photographs of him, and through his huge influence, no one who has anything to do with yoga is unaffected by this man, and his hallmark is the leonine passion and commitment to his art. Every cell of his being is focused in every yoga posture – as is movingly evident in even the poorest black and white photograph of him out of focus at the other end of a room – he literally embodies his own search for meaning. Even indirect contact with such a leader cannot leave one unmoved. It challenges one's own compromises and shows just what is possible in a fully and courageously committed life.

I *do* have direct contact with a remarkable teacher of the Korean martial art Tae Kwon Do. Tae Kwon Do is constantly struggling with its own internal politics. Students of Tae Kwon Do disappear, reappear, come and go, according to the counter-pressures of their studies, their careers, their relationships. It never feels like a very stable group or a very stable organizational structure. All these troubles are forgotten, however, as soon as this teacher starts to teach. Even if you were not remotely interested in Tae Kwon Do you would find him interesting to watch because, like Mr Iyengar, every move he makes is as perfect as it could be at that particular moment. That total discipline makes him exceptional. I was interested to hear, in a similar vein, a member of the Berlin Philharmonic Orchestra comment that their conductor, Claudio Abbado *embodies* whatever music they are working on: 'His whole person *becomes* the music.' That complete intellectual *and* physical involvement seems to be the hallmark of that particularly intense charisma.

Nobody can *decide* to become charismatic. On the other hand, it is not simply a question of 'you're born with it or you're not', either. We can see that getting fully involved with the task and being fully committed to the ideas and the organization you are engaged with creates an energy field of its own. A self-conscious attempt to develop charisma would probably have disastrous results but allowing whatever ignites your interest in work to take your full attention may generate that atmosphere of confidence and positivity around you. If you are concerned to become more charismatic, a route towards it is in fact to become deeply involved in what you are doing. Otherwise you are involved in a quest which is similar to saying 'how can I be more creative?' These butterflies cannot be netted.

Charisma used simply to glorify the ego of its owner was *not* valued by colleagues, and in fact was seen as a destructive force (see p. 21). Everyone who valued charismatic leaders emphasized that their charisma was also backed by good organization and shaped by a clear vision, be it commercial or ideological, and was balanced by consummate practical skill.

Energizing leadership

The charismatic leader creates a particular kind of energy and a particular spur to review one's own life and achievements. As a role model, a charismatic leader is both inspiring and daunting. One will not meet many in a lifetime.

An energizing leader may be easier to find, and easier to be, if we look on energizing leading as a way of forming a creative alliance.

'The best leader I've ever had', says Joan Yates, a 42-year-old senior university lecturer:

> is my current head of department. His main quality is his ability to get alongside people. He doesn't tell people what to do, but identifies things that need to be done, and does them with them. He gives people their own space.

The skill of 'getting alongside people' may be particularly important if you have a talented and motivated team. With considerable self-knowledge, Joan says:

> I respond badly to being told what to do: I start to make leadership bids myself. It motivates me a lot to have somebody who doesn't set himself up as the expert, and doesn't need to be everybody's favourite person. Brian is not uncritical, he does point out when you could do things better. He has high expectations of everyone and constantly encourages people. His message is 'You can do it!'

In fact, she says that contact with this leader has had a very positive effect on her: 'I've attempted to do things I wouldn't have thought possible', and indeed she has achieved both significant promotion, an international profile and publication, during the period of this person's leadership.

At the age of forty-nine, Mark Ellis runs a community school. Ten years ago, as a science teacher who wanted to put an integrated science programme into practice and run a radical science department which really knew what it was doing, he enjoyed an energizing form of leadership from his head.

> He had a remarkable combination of people leadership and a clear view of the task. Although he was clear, he didn't force his vision on people, he explored things with people, with consummate skill.

That good alliance motivated Mark just as it did Joan,

> I was always a hard worker, but I wanted to work harder. He supported you – I always felt supported. Even when I made mistakes I felt supported.

A team member who wants to create and innovate will be particularly appreciative of this energizing leadership which supports and assists in structuring their creative activity without taking it over. Credit where credit is due remains a point of great importance; few manoeuvres induce more bitterness than that which Joan describes from a previous boss: 'His time was spent either doing his own thing or claiming glory from other people's activities.'

Great competence can be energizing in itself. Sian Smith remembers a school teacher whom:

> I think of with great affection because she used to come through the door firing from the hip! We used every one of the forty minutes every time. Also, the subject was Latin which was deeply satisfying because you can actually get Latin completely right. It's one of the few subjects where you can get 100% and you can get into a lovely logical flow. But what I remember is this teacher coming in totally organized, totally informed, knowing exactly what we were going to do for every second of the class, and I found it really quite exhilarating!

Empathy and judgement delicately combined make the best sort of energizing leadership, as well as a clear commitment to allowing people to go on owning their own ideas and any glory which follows from those ideas being put into practice.

Developing leadership

A leader who allows her or his staff space to develop, and who has good insight into how to promote that development, is much valued by staff. The development might be personal: Simon Ayres values his present boss who 'keeps me safe from my own anger by preventing me from getting cross with him'.

This is not an exercise in oppression, but a perceptive reaction. Simon finds his anger can often be a disorganizing force:

> I get into a muddle with anger. My anger is always more powerful than I think – I'm always amazed how much it upsets people.

Thus a leader who helps him to avoid an angry reaction altogether, is an assistance.

The developmental aspect may be technical or professional:

> He's always there if I want him but he doesn't interfere. That

was especially true when I first started this job. He always made me feel it was OK to ask him for information even if it was three times a day.

Parminder Sharma is Corporate Management Development Officer in a national broadcasting org. She has a clear sense that to promote your development, the person who leads you needs to be someone who has insight about their own boundaries. She feels that she herself is:

> sensitive to the energies around me. My boss works fast and has a macro not a micro vision. He is very skilled and I get a lot of my own development from watching him, learn by osmosis, pick things up. He provides guidance and boundaries and an environment in which it's safe for me to take risks, and that's what I need: someone who offers me a bit more than I've got myself.

Her point about boundaries is important: you need to know yourself pretty well to be strong enough to allow your staff to develop without feeling threatened. However feeling threatened is often correct and appropriate in corporate life. Your friend probably is after your job. Your secretary probably would like to supersede you. Your colleagues' political game-plan may well include your removal.

The macho response to this would be to block everyone's development and network at every point. Sometimes that may be necessary. However, there are often alternatives, for instance, in facilitating your staff's development, which will improve everybody's skills and abilities and give them greater job satisfaction, while you keep a calm and assertive eye on anything political which is emerging.

You also need considerable interpersonal skills to be able to push someone to extend their potential without pushing them over the edge. Phoebe Driscoll, Operations Manager at a national employment agency says:

> I think that an element of discomfort is important in good leadership and good staff development, but that people need to be challenged constantly rather than threatened constantly.

She also sees a key part of the developmental role as genuine delegation, drawing this useful distinction:

> If you get an absolutely clear definition of roles, then you can make sure that your staff are making genuine *decisions* and not just *recommendations*. They are then truly accountable for those decisions and take the credit if things go well and the reverse if things go badly. If it's not clearly defined, the decisions don't really belong to anybody.

Cara Frances's long experience in publishing leads her to a similar conclusion.

> My best boss so far was someone who delegated and then had confidence in the people she delegated to. She let you have your head and go. But then I always felt if something turned out to be total rubbish I could go back to her and say, where have I gone wrong? This increased my confidence, it gave me an ability to try, to get a sense of achievement, but also to consult back without feeling I had failed.

And Julia Primera (thirty-eight, Personnel Specialist), agrees:

> The best leadership I've experienced was from a man who was participative, supportive, and made you feel worthwhile and enthusiastic. He gave me lots of freedom and trusted me to do what needed to be done.

We can see from these comments that a knowledge of our own strengths is what we need to become assured enough to allow our team members to grow into their own strengths as fully as possible.

Unconventional leadership

Every now and again a truly unconventional leader may come our way. As Leonard Rawlins found, it is an enriching experience when it works well.

> I worked for a director once who was very hard to be with at a human level; lots of people wanted to strangle her. However,

she brought to that organization what was right for it at that time. She made sure actions were the result of *clear thinking* whereas the organization had a long history of woolly thinking and internal politicking. Marie was completely free of internal politics. Her creative thinking was good too, her 'What about this?' suggestions were always insightful and helpful.

What Marie managed to do was remain very focused on the task – to get the organization back on the rails – without having any of her energy drawn into playing office politics or wanting everyone to like her. She thus came over as something of a maverick, but her talent and effectiveness turned the organization round.

It may be worth noticing that sometimes the task must be central and paramount, and other considerations such as popularity and infighting set aside, however unconventional it may make you appear. If you have worked well with unconventional leaders, you will probably notice, on reflection, that their apparent oddness was because they were so focused on their task that they were not observing some of the surface forms. Our stereotype of the 'absent-minded professor' or the 'mad artist' shows that culturally we allow that some activities can be completely absorbing. Maybe our work practices would change for the better if we could extend the spectrum of jobs and projects where we feel that sense of total absorption is appropriate.

There are lots of ways of not falling into the macho trap that everybody knows about from the 1980s. These examples illustrate that there are many different ways of managing successfully which do not follow the macho model, however 'traditional' that began to seem in the last decade. Having spent some time exploring what the many qualities embodying *good* leadership might be, let us look at the elements – and costs – of *bad* leadership.

TRIGGER TWO:
Ask yourself: What is the worst leadership I have experienced?
What were the qualities and style of that leadership and what effect did it have on me?

When people talk about their good leaders, they get a faraway look in their eyes, speak rather slowly, and seem to be enjoying revisiting and reviewing the positive experience they have had. When they speak about the bad leaders they have worked with, in contrast, a fiendish animation comes into them. They speak quickly, gesticulate, thump the table, raise their voices, and their eyes shine with an angry glitter.

What do we learn from this simple fact? We learn that people really *hate* being badly led, they hate the unfairness, the waste of energy, the amazingly pervasive mess that a mismanaging senior person can make in an organization. We also learn that bad leadership in the workplace can demoralize a person in all aspects of their life, because anyone who feels their energy is being mischannelled into futile ends at work, or is being deviously or unfairly treated at work, feels out of equilibrium and under stress in their personal life as well. As a society we are becoming more and more aware of the catastrophe of abuse in our society, at the extremes of sexual and political abuse. We need to look too at the less lurid but still important abuses of bad leadership in corporate and organizational life.

Afraid of the job

We may experience bad leadership because our boss is afraid of his or her job. We need to notice that insecurity about our own performance can undermine our capacity to lead well. Cara once worked for:

> someone who was afraid of her own position. She was inclined to be belittling and expect me to be upset if criticized. When she had a go at me one day she eventually said, 'Aren't you going to cry?' because her practice was to reduce people to tears. She sensed she had reached her own ceiling and was minding her back in order not to be overtaken.

Tears may be a constructive expression at times. Women *and* men cry at work, and away from work about work, far more than we realize. However, it is hard to see how causing someone to cry simply in order to feel power over them or to compensate for your own sense of powerlessness is justifiable. If you feel a growing impulse in yourself to handle situations by upsetting people, take a step back and rethink. There is an immediate relief in behaving like this but the long-term costs are high – people leave their jobs, concentrate on something else, or become unproductive, and direct their energy elsewhere. They certainly lose respect for you.

If you find yourself lashing out, recall to yourself how you would like other people to perceive you – as someone who is strong in themselves, rather than someone who throws their weight around in a bullying manner.

Simon Ayres also worked for someone who:

> felt out of her depth in her job. She was trying to be macho. For the first six weeks that she was in the post I never saw her at all, she was nipping round the great and the good, to see what wisdom they had to impart. She didn't delegate, she dumped responsibility, and we felt scapegoated all the time. We thought we were an advisory body and then she tried to blame us for never taking decisions.

Clear lines of accountability and explicit delegation show up again as key issues, but so too does a sense of someone trying to ingratiate themselves with the kings and queens without even getting to know their own team members. Notice any times you may have fallen into that pattern yourself – and any occasions when your leader has behaved in that way.

Hiding behind the job

Job titles have great mythological power. How would you like to be able to introduce yourself at parties? Financial Director? Doctor? Secretary? Teacher? Housewife or househusband? Accountant? Dancer? How would you react to meeting someone with each of those roles? Do you slightly draw yourself up to attention for an F.D. and start wanting to gauge their real clout by finding out the size of their company? Do you assume that househusbands are green-voting New Men and secretaries interchangeable helpmeets? Maybe, like many people, you feel an automatic semi-cringe towards doctors, and a slight alarm about anyone in the creative professions.

Accountants will be funny or important depending on your age (pre- or post-Monty Python). Or maybe your mind-set is altogether different and you react in ways quite other than those I have described, but the chances are you do react in some way to a job title – either by being impressed or by marginally writing them off.

Let us look at how certain kinds of poor leadership can feed off the aura of the job title as a substitute for any genuine effort on their part:

> This woman relied on her position to give her status, not her own behaviour. She was a vulgar, foulmouthed person who just said, 'you have to respect my position' when in fact there was no shape to the organization, no code to fall back on, all in all a moral vacuum. (Neil Glover)

Authority can be used to cover up untruths:

> I worked for a man once who was enormously charismatic, he could hold the whole audience of the Albert Hall in the palm of his hand, but I knew that some of what he was saying was based on lies. It was very disturbing. He inspired huge numbers of people to do things, and yet he was very manipulative.
>
> Once, for reasons of internal politics, he wanted to make a particular appointment and said that we had to select candidate X because he was the only person who spoke language Y. It was some months before we realized that language Y did not exist! (Leonard Rawlins)

This breathtaking disregard for honesty is certainly a challenge. It may be a way that a colleague or boss gauges your strength and integrity by seeing what you will do. Will you raise the question? Have you ever used the authority of your job to push something through under a cloak of misleading information or actual untruth? Many times one might feel that the end justifies the means but, as well as the moral question of whether it is really acceptable behaviour, there is the serious question of how other members of the team feel if they find out. Have you ever had a sense that someone senior to you was using the 'magic' of their position to do something which was in the last analysis dishonest? How did you feel about it when they did?

Non-leadership

A rather extreme form of hiding behind the name of the job, is simply not to do the job at all, and a surprising number of people seem to be sitting in surprisingly senior posts, not actually performing in any way whatever.

> My boss appears to lead from the front – that is he wades in, he does a fourteen-hour day six and a half days a week. However, to him, going through the motions is more important than analysing actions. He deals with the minutiae but he doesn't really steer the ship.
>
> On top of that he's unable to give praise, he lacks warmth, he's got poor socializing ability and poor interface with subordinates. This breeds a nasty, bitching environment. (Derek Crispin)

This sounds like more or less a full house on leadership failure! None of the leadership functions are going well, to the extent that the man can hardly be said to be doing the job at all.

Some non-leadership is a kind of utter intellectual banality, where no effort is made to form any kind of vision at all. Mark Ellis headed up a science department in a school during the time when the 'single sciences' issue demanded enormous re-thinking and upheaval. 'My boss only called one staff meeting during that period,' he says, 'and that was to inform us of correct procedure with board rubbers.'

Joan Yates felt a similarly rudderless leadership lowered her energy and output for months:

> I withdrew, and felt confirmed in a view of myself that I couldn't achieve anything. I lost all desire to move forwards.

Sean McCann, a partner in an accountancy firm says:

The indecisiveness and intellectual dishonesty of the leaders in my firm is obvious to those led. It really undermines your own process.

Part of the brief for being a leader has to be to take the risk of forming the vision, to take the risk of setting the structure and owning responsibility for the team or the organization's direction. We feel we are pouring energy into a pointless bottomless pit when we are not led. Not-leading when we should be leading is a horrible experience – one feels completely out of control. Passivity is damaging to both parties and is something we need to notice and respond to, whether it be in ourselves or in others.

Manipulative leadership

Parminder found one of the men she used to work for extremely manipulative:

He was divisive, sexist and racist. He could not set up systems to empower the staff. The whole experience was awful, it was like being down an empty well. I felt there was no way out, I would be stuck there forever. I became confrontational – it was the only way I could survive.

A divide–and–rule style can indeed spark off aggression eventually. Divisiveness is not the only way of being manipulative. Trying to ingratiate yourself with people without any real positive intent is another. Julia was at the receiving end in one of her roles: 'My boss was not domineering, he was oily unctuous. He seemed deferential but he was in fact underhand. I left the job because of him,' she says, adding darkly, 'I should have known what he was like when he gave me a teddy bear for Christmas.'

She gives us the clue there to the fact that manipulative behaviour is not easy immediately to detect, and one may go along for a number of weeks or months with a horrible feeling that something is wrong without being able to say precisely what it is.

Janet King found the same thing about a colleague of hers:

It took me three to six months to decode this because the man was very diffident, but I worked out eventually that he was arbitrary and he was manipulative. He had no systems and he had no procedures. Everything was done on the old boy network. *I am not an old boy.*

Many women and some men will share her deep annoyance on that final point.

Manipulating people, through dishonesty, through flattery, through appearing to work transparently, but actually working to private rules and values (such as the 'old boy network'), may win some short-term gains in terms of getting some specific results that you want; however, the build-up of resentment is quick, and you lose staff loyalty and commitment and sometimes actually the staff themselves.

Ask yourself whether you do ever lead your team manipulatively. It is hard to admit it, but manipulative behaviour is very easy to slip into as a matter of expediency, or as a slippage from *strategic* thinking and work. Perhaps being manipulative does seem to you to be justified or necessary, but it is worth regularly reminding yourself what the costs may be in terms of lost trust, lost respect, and lost integrity.

Inconsistent values

Cara's further comment on her manipulative boss is this:

> She had bitten off more than she could chew, so she couldn't brief me properly. Being over-promoted and not at ease with her own position, she couldn't give a clear picture of what she wanted. The goal posts kept moving.

Inconsistent leadership infuriates, depowers and demotivates people. They feel a pervasive insanity in their lives and a ludicrous unfairness. It does great damage and causes staff to want to move to escape. Mark Ellis had a horrible time with one of his previous bosses who was:

> Inconsistent to an unbelievable degree. You never knew from one moment to the next whether she would be laughing or crying, whether you were going to get a profound comment

or a demand for you to support her. There was real malice in this woman and some of her deeds and since I was her deputy, I often had to repair the damage she had done. I'm scarred for life, [he says, finishing sombrely] I'm not joking.

The stress and strain of coping with her behaviour is something he will never forget.

Phoebe Driscoll is angered by inconsistency in leadership because it is so difficult to stop it compromising the quality of one's own work:

Inconsistency of standards is impossible to work around, because it's very contaminating. You are the conduit for information and systems, and so inevitably *your* message becomes inconsistent too.

If you have worked with an inconsistent leader you probably have vivid memories of your dismay at each volte-face, and if you are in that situation now you probably have some weary strategy for coping. It is extremely important to remember, once in a leadership role oneself, the desperation caused to staff by chopping and changing and moving the goalposts. Sometimes it would be easier to allow some movement in aims and objectives but it should never happen without discussion, consultation and agreement, or your staff's commitment, capacity for optimism and quite probably their health too, are forfeit.

Problems with team-building

A leader who is effective and fair needs to have developed his or her concept of teams. What is a team, how should it bond, how should the dynamics work, what size should it be, should it grow or stay the same size, should the roles develop, and so forth: all these questions must be addressed and can be answered in a variety of positive ways.

A leader who cannot, or chooses not to build a team, will be resented and engender negative feeling among staff. 'Divide and rule' may be appealing as a short term response to a problem, but generates cynicism in the end.

Eleven years ago one of our Division Heads, had, we realized later, his own interests at heart. He took us along avenues that were not right for the corporate point. He was looking at increasing turnover without a future, and this was to do with building his own empire. It took a while for us to realize it. (Derek Britton)

Angela recalls working for an unbalanced team which had:

too many chiefs and not enough Indians. This created a lack of responsibility chains and communication chains; management was by consensus. One of the worst débâcles I saw was a decision regarding a redundancy where the bad news filtered down through the ranks, and eventually everyone knew about it except the person concerned. Everyone was *very* uncomfortable.

Academic institutions have struggled during the last decade to get to grips with management issues and somehow to integrate them with issues of intellectual honesty. There has been a massive upheaval in the culture and networks, both official and unofficial, which form the texture of academic life. A nineteenth-century sense of scholarly excellence is no longer the most compelling criterion where ancient institutions now have to compete for funding in a ruthless market-place, and the definitions of scholarly excellence and scholarly responsibility have changed so radically anyway that enormous amounts of time and energy are spent endeavouring to understand what they are.

When institutional values change like this there is genuine anguish caused to employees. There is a period when the two cultures are fighting for supremacy within the institution. It goes beyond what seems like 'work' because people choose the job they choose because they feel coherent with the value system it embodies.

Surviving a profound cultural change in your organization means you need to:

- recognize that it is a major crisis and respect the fact that it will have a big effect on you.
- emphasize good 'time out': really be sure you have relaxing and absorbing leisure interludes.

- express your own points to influence the change with detached assertiveness, *not* passionate aggression.

No one who works in industry and commerce can expect to escape a similar radical upset in aims and values in the next ten years. Chronic recession has eroded our industrial base in the UK, and the crisis in primary and secondary education has eroded our skills base. Creating work and success with just those two challenges would be bad enough, but the planet itself is finally driven to the verge of collapse by our reckless use of resources this century. In this context feasible and appropriate business behaviour will be one of the key, urgent concepts to define. Universities may thus have useful information and insights to share concerning deeply upsetting shifts and changes in attitudes, policy and actions.

To hold a team together at such a time one senior lecturer explains that the essential leadership quality is vision. He deplores the lack of vision at his own place of work:

> All our professors have been disastrous. The first one never talked to anyone except his cronies, so that the department became polarized into two camps. He wasn't particularly polarized himself, he just had *no* conception of where the department was going at all.
>
> The other chair was held by a woman who was desperate to be liked, desperate to make alliances, so she made alliances with the people who were most approachable, who were the younger members of staff. Our current professor has taken against various people, which makes me uncomfortable. I don't want someone bland, but I do want someone who has respect for people and some idea where he thinks things are going. (Paul Norton)

Domineering leadership

The most blatant 'macho' behaviour in leadership style is a clear 'domineering' line. It is not the same as producing and communicating a good clear structure, and in fact is often the reverse. Sean McCann says 'There is bullying and disrespect from those in

charge in my office. It goes with a general indecisiveness.'
Janet King found that:

> I had a boss at one time whose attitude was rigidly formal.
> Everything was structured to a degree that was very daunting
> and there was no scope whatever. His style was didactic and
> bewildering.

Michael Groves found that the old-style academic concept of
leadership was cold and domineering:

> The academic attitude which comes from archaeology at
> Cambridge is 'fend for yourself'! You get given a directive to
> do something which has no obvious end product, there's no
> good reason for you to do it and no thought given to how your
> findings will be implemented. You're simply given a topic
> and *no* help.

These three comments highlight the sources that a domineering
style might arise from: in the first case in order to cover up an
incompetence in the management, in the second place to curtail
the development of a member of staff, and in the third place to try
to make the management position look like delegation when it is
in fact pure neglect. What is not in question is that staff become
alienated and demotivated when treated in this way.

Leadership review

You will now have thought through your own experiences of
good and bad leadership, and will have had ideas sparked off by
the other experiences you have read. It is useful to sum up in your
own mind what your thinking on leadership is now. This does
not have to be a policy statement which remains fixed for months
or years into the future – it can be part of a new and exploratory
piece of thinking on your part. Re-think whenever you need to,
and try new things out.

Yin and yang

We have seen that the wanted and valued leader is sometimes a giver and sometimes a receiver, sometimes firm and sometimes flexible, sometimes hectic and sometimes quiet.

There are masculine and feminine qualities but they do not necessarily equate to men and women. In English this is a linguistic confusion we have to live with, so frequently in this book I have used the Chinese terms *yin* and *yang*. Yin is the dark side of the mountain and yang is the light side. The two flow together in the yin-yang sign as a symbol of the eternal flow of energy from one aspect of life to another – from day to night, from cold to warm, from high to low, loud to quiet, birth to death, all the opposites which the universe holds. In each part of the symbol is a dot of the opposite colour. This represents the fact that everything contains the seed of its opposite. In day is the potential for the next night, in winter, the seed of the next summer, and so on.

Yin is often taken to be a symbol for 'feminine' qualities and yang for 'masculine' qualities. Everyone, male or female, needs to work out what their own balance of yin and yang is. 'Macho' management, in the sense of management that leans heavily on

yang qualities and excludes yin qualities, is bound, in these terms, to be out of balance.

Experiment with this diagram – write into the yang section all the *desirable* leadership qualities that you would tend to classify as 'masculine', and in the yin section, all the leadership qualities you would tend to assign as 'feminine'. Notice what the balance is like, whether some qualities are difficult to assign one way or another. Note any new points that arise for you as you work on this.

If you think in terms of feminism the masculine/feminine split may irritate you – instead think of yang being open, obvious, daylight qualities and yin being subtle, complex, 'in the dark' qualities and make your divisions on that basis.

Baggage

Here is another diagram to write in.

As you have progressed through this chapter you will have qualities or pieces of behaviour that you are quite clear you never want to engage in. Write them into the bag and then view this bag as the excess baggage you plan never to take with you again!

Action

You may have felt inspired, agitated, or otherwise inclined by what you have read and thought, to take some action right now. If so, take some time to write yourself an action plan. Good action planning is specific, achievable and time-targeted. Tell yourself exactly what, exactly how, and exactly when you intend to do something, and you will find it very much easier to do.

It might be an action that is very outward and involved with work practices, or it might be an inner adjustment you wish to make, but take time to notice it while it is vivid in your mind.

2. Gut feelings

If you did the 'yin-yang' exercise at the end of chapter 1 you might well have written 'intuition' in the yin space. You might also have put 'being a good listener' or 'being good at dealing with people' in the yin space, and maybe 'giving clear instructions', 'knowing when to say "no" ', or 'keeping high standards of work', on the yang side.

Gut feelings may seem riskily unprofessional. They do however enhance to a critical degree your ability to understand the implications of information. This will mean that you will be a more effective manager because you will prioritize properly and you will avoid time-wasting misunderstandings. At the end of the day this means that more and better work gets done.

That whole cluster of skills is of course communication and interpersonal work in both its yin and its yang aspect. Maybe a huge groan rises in your gorge at the words 'communication' and 'inter-personal'. Perhaps you feel saturated with irrelevant psychobabble about both. If you do, I sympathize, but nevertheless suggest that the subject remains important for the simple reason that it still so often goes wrong. 'Are you in pain?' said a paediatrician to a pale and unnaturally still child who had just undergone surgery. 'No,' said the child. After a moment she said, 'Excuse me', to the doctor. 'Yes?' he said. 'Does "pain" mean when it hurts?' asked the child. This upsetting example shows just how important it is that we are being as clear with one another as we think we are.

Let us look first at communication *in* and at communication *out* – that is, at what we need to *receive* in the way of information, impressions and feedback, and what we need to *convey* in the sense of instructions, guidelines, and requests and reports.

Communications in

We can receive information from staff on three different levels: by verbal report, by observation and by intuition. Our sense may be that verbal report is a rather masculine and open way to communicate, where intuition might be a more subtle, more feminine skill. The divisions are not quite so clear, however, because 'hearing' what another person is saying can be done passively or actively, empathetically or aggressively, and the quality of information exchanged will vary a great deal accordingly. We will look at moving from an opaque 'macho' style where only the words said are, as it were, admissible evidence, and not the way in which they are said or the hidden agendas that they may carry. This is not to say that every exchange could or should be a therapy session, but simply to point out that a Cartesian idea of objective truth is sometimes confused with what is in fact a failure of imagination.

TRIGGER THREE:

> *What kind of information from your staff do you regard as most important?*

What do you need to know, and how might you best be sure that you know it? Neil Glover says he needs 'quick, accurate feedback about cock-ups'; Phoebe Driscoll says, 'anything at all that directly affects business', while David Britton simply says, 'the truth'.

Let us look at these categories one at a time. It is important to everyone that 'information about cock-ups' gets passed up the line as quickly and efficiently as possible. Neil is echoed by Cara Frances who says:

> I want to create a climate where it is possible to understand where my staff are with things, so that if performance is not up to strength I know why.

Angela Winters also emphasizes the need to be clear what staff can and cannot do:

> I have experienced delegating something to junior staff believing that I had explained what to do – and they said they

did understand, but it transpired that they didn't understand at all. I do need staff to be honest about their inability to do a task, but it is a two-way process because you have to make it possible for them to tell you.

The 'two-way process' and 'creating a climate' are crucial. A manager who reacts with aggression or panic to bad news risks creating a climate where staff put off reporting problems because they fear the explosion that will ensue. It is worth noticing what one feels one needs to do to be a leader who both expects high standards *and* is able to listen calmly to a staff member saying, 'I don't understand', 'I've made a mistake', or 'I don't know what to do next' – and furthermore to react constructively.

Does a manager need to be able to discuss staff's personal problems or not? Although it is important not to deny the fact that staff have other parts of their life away from the workplace and that respect and space must be accorded to those, it is not compulsory to be deeply entangled in their private lives to be a good empathetic manager. Being aware of what your boundaries are and communicating that well, is an important element of management for many people.

Siobhan Boyle worries that her own consummate skills may make her unapproachable:

It happens regularly that people find me so competent and able that they fear they'll look stupid if they talk to me. I'd hate to think my staff couldn't come to me with work *or* personal problems – I'd hate it if they felt I was too far away or too aloof. There is a certain level of truth in the idea that if you do listen, you're a 'soft touch'. It's hard in terms of getting people to still take responsibility for themselves.

Phoebe is clear she only wants to know if it *is* an issue that affects work, and not if it does not.

Paul is clear that he needs to know:

how they feel about what they're doing. That means it's important they talk about what *is* working as well as what *isn't*.

When you first arrive in an organization or department it may be useful to take Mark Ellis's line and say, 'I'm interested in anything at all that you want to tell me' – a genuine open-door policy giving him a chance to gather a huge informal database, particularly in the early weeks of his appointment, when, hopeful for change and with histories to get off their chests, staff are bound to be particularly open.

At a later stage of an appointment you may move more into Janet King's position, which is:

> I want to be kept informed, but not of *everything*, because that would undermine delegation. If something has gone particularly well I want to know so that we can celebrate it and mention it in the right places and if something's gone particularly badly, I want to know because I might pick up flack and need to know how to counter it, or I might need to take remedial action. I like people to let me know about initiatives, or possibilities, or scope for exceptional response.

We need to be careful to know everything we need to, but not get swamped unnecessarily with excess work-data, or other people's emotional housework. Reflect on how you manage to select what you need to know, and what information can flow on downstream without you.

David Britton homes in on how you make sure that what your staff give you is indeed 'the truth' – 'It all comes down to relationships.'

He visualizes these relationships with his managers all over Europe as:

> strong dotted lines. I need to know things like early warnings that things don't feel quite right, for example if the financial viability of a customer is uncertain. I need them to respect me and be able to talk to me.

Leonard Rawlins has an insight about a particular kind of truth which may slip away:

> I want to know the reality of what's going on with the client and the product. The higher up an organization you get, the more protected you are from that sort of truth. In one of my

jobs I went and worked half a day a week in each department until I'd got right round. I cleaned fridges, I did anything, and that was a *real* eye-opener.

'Walking the job', in your own persona or incognito, may be an important way of getting the information you want. You might have qualms about getting information under 'false pretences' if you visit different branches without revealing your identity, or you might feel it is important enough to you to get to hear the unvarnished truth, for the means to justify the ends.

Active listening

You can extend the amount of accurate information that is passed onto you by your staff by developing the art of active listening. 'I've worked and worked at listening,' says Leonard feelingly, 'I really have.'

A number of strands come together in active listening. At first we need to practise them as deliberate 'methods', but eventually they coalesce into a natural way to behave. It is the same point noted by Howard Reid in the section on the soft martial art Pa Kua in *The Way of Harmony* (Unwin Paperbacks, 1988):

> Although it is true that when you learn Pa Kua you must initially take its form and structure into your movements, the main aim – which Pa Kua shares with all other soft arts, – is the ultimate loss of form.

– that is, technique eventually merges so completely with your behaviour that it is no longer a separate 'form'.

Strands we could usefully look at are:

- not having all the 'air time'
- creating a listening silence
- not interrupting
- clarifying bad news assertively
- prompting for good news
- closing well: react consistently and honourably

Taking all the 'air time' is rather macho acquisitive behaviour. We may have been well rewarded for it in the past, and used it as a way of coming top at school and college, getting attention in a junior pool of workers, displaying potential and ambition, making leadership bids, exhibiting general intellectual pyrotechnics. When you want and need information from your staff though, it is a counterproductive style to use. It is very inhibiting for the person you are talking to. The trick is to stop thinking of talking being 'active' and listening being 'passive', and to get hold of the thought that by listening well you are being very active indeed. Once you get a sense that you can have a quiet centre of equilibrium and power inside yourself, you do not need to impact on the occasion by hearing your own voice running all the way through it. In fact, there is probably at least one person in your life about whom people say 'She (or he) doesn't say much, but when she (he) does say something, it's really worth hearing.' You can increase the effect of what you say by saying less: it is not a risk to do so.

Creating a listening silence means being receptive in body and mind. If your spiritual side is important to you, it means being receptive in spirit too. Make steady, but intermittent eye contact with the person with whom you are talking: an unwavering glare never empowered anybody to open up or express themselves, but unpressurizing and calm eye contact is essential. Be careful not to look away if the tension increases or a controversial subject is mentioned. Keep your body language relaxed and alert. Do not slump but do not tense up either. Keep equal weight in each hip, lift your spine and the crown of your head up, and release your shoulders down. Try to avoid crossing your legs very tightly or folding your arms very tightly. Keep your joints reasonably loose. Do the same with your facial muscles: simply try to keep them smooth.

Most powerfully of all, breathe slowly and steadily. The more you control your breathing, the more the other person will relax and speak their mind. The deep animal signal of you breathing steadily – a little more slowly than usual and allowing the breath right down into the hips – is that you are strong and relaxed, you can handle anything the other person tells you, you are not going to go off the deep end, you are going to listen and respond in a measured and constructive way.

People have told me truly *incredible* things, simply, I am convinced, because I practised creating a listening silence, and particularly practised controlling my breathing. I never set out to trick anybody into telling me anything, but have been the recipient of a great deal of 'highly classified' material in my time, because of this practice.

Not interrupting follows on naturally from the first two points. It is all too easy, when someone tries to explain something, to say 'Oh yes, that happened to me when . . .', or 'Last time that happened we did . . .' or 'If I were you I would . . .'. These kinds of responses belong to social conversation. In the work context they are usually a distraction and a tangent, and only rarely a valid illustration that will move things on. Your staff member needs to tell you what is happening for him, not to be regaled by your past glories. He needs to work out what *he* should do, not listen to what you would do in his place. It is useful to make encouraging noises: 'mm', 'yes', 'I see', 'of course', and so on, as appropriate. Gauge delicately how often you need to make a small sound like this so that the other person does not feel isolated. Do not go into a trance and think about something else while interjecting little phrases – this is as insulting as the deadly marital 'yes, dear'!

Basic assertiveness helps in clarifying the bad news a person is trying to tell you, and in prompting for good news. Simply make calm, clear, and assertive prompts if someone is incoherent because they are tense and fearful:

- 'Take your time'

is a very useful message to give. So is,

- 'Is there anything else you'd like to say about this?'
- 'Do you think there's anything else I ought to know?'

All these prompts help to get a full account of any bad news a colleague wants to pass on. It is also useful to prompt calmly and assertively for positive news:

- 'What have you been pleased about at work recently?'
- 'What's been the best achievement this week?'
- 'What can we celebrate at the moment?'

Especially in UK culture it remains difficult to talk about our successes – we are so thoroughly conditioned not to 'show off'. However, it is strengthening and encouraging to put one's successes into words, share them, and be appreciated for them. You can improve your staff's energy and morale by inviting them regularly to speak positively about themselves.

Finishing well and reacting well makes it more likely that you will actually get information from your staff again. Obviously it is helpful to finish the conversation on a positive note if possible. It is certainly useful to finish with a *specific* point of planning or intent if you can:

- 'Well I think the first thing I shall do is . . .'
- 'We will finalize that by the end of the week . . .'

inspire more confidence than the general:

- 'Leave it with me . . .'

The final part of active listening is perhaps the most important of all. We have already seen how important it is to be consistent (p. 23), but you may have choked on the idea of 'acting honourably' as completely unrealistic where you work, where an ability to think and act strategically may be at a premium. Power broking and power games are a large part of many people's working lives. I remember a doctor I was talking with falling about laughing when I said to him, 'But I thought hospitals were places for healing people in.' 'No, no,' he said, 'they're places for doctors to fight one another in.'

Information may have to be used selectively and thoughtfully, and there are few organizations in which it is safe to be utterly transparent and open. Nevertheless, we can be aware of not *abusing* information entrusted to us, not using it against the person giving the information, or in a way that they strongly do not want. If there is an unavoidable conflict of interest here, we can at least be careful to explain how and why we feel we must use their report in the way in which we intend to. Without such measures they will be unlikely to pass on, for example, 'quick accurate information about cock-ups', again.

Observation

There is some information that comes one's way as a manager, which is not material one is told, but material one has observed. Michael Groves feels he is particularly well-trained to be observant and that observant behaviour is common in his profession.

> Being observant just means being sensitive to *all* the signs you see around you. Don't rationalize yourself into believing anything because that is what your preconception is. Archaeology is a more introspective profession than most. We work by a process of deduction, and have a strong element of training in observation.

It is interesting to think how paying attention to minutiae may allow one, like an archaeologist, to form an accurate and complex deduction about what is really going on. Some professional disciplines incline one to be more observant and deductive than others, but Michael's key point is: 'Be sensitive to *all* the signs.'

Parminder cites a case where this was important for her:

> I went away, and on my return my assistant said 'Welcome back', but her body language said 'Piss off' – I did talk to her about it, and found out what was bugging her.

Chris Hargreaves sees some of his deductive activity on the crossover between objective observation and subjective intuition:

> I don't think I act on blind hunches, but I am subjective in working and whether I believe someone else's judgement, or should trust their advice. It comes back to a feeling that is usually based on having absorbed information.

Julia Primera, on the other hand, feels under pressure to clothe her intuition with a logical gloss:

> I often believe or know things without knowing how I know them, or even being interested in how I know them. I do wonder if it is accurate data gathering – I'm very good at

picking up signals. If challenged though I can quickly generate a rationale and say it with conviction and dignity.

Developing observation

Developing your skills in observation can be done in a gradual way. It is a matter of taking Michael Groves's point and becoming sensitive to 'all the signals'. Forming a habit of noticing proxemics (how people have chosen to distribute themselves in the room), body language, tone, pitch and speed of voice. It is a process of learning *not* to dismiss the evidence that comes to you subliminally in these ways, not disregarding such sensibility as too feminine, too yin, to be worth attending to. Learn to declassify material from 'it's probably just my imagination' to 'it's invaluable non-verbal information that can help me form a clear picture of what is going on'.

Intuition

Another layer down from acute observation is pure intuition. Intuition is certainly not thought of as macho and is frequently expressed in the cliché 'feminine intuition', and yet is a crucial resource for many women and men in business.

Phoebe Driscoll is vigorous in her defence of intuition as an everyday necessary function:

> We have a tendency today to talk about skills all the time as qualities we can acquire, and of course that's quite right, but we are foolish to negate all the 'old' skills like intuition. Intuition is rarely wrong, and when it is it isn't a problem. I don't expect a 100% success rate from any skill so why should I expect a 100% success rate from intuition?

Our move towards good Equal Opportunities thinking rightly makes us question anything that could be called an 'innate' quality, but in the case of intuition we need to consider whether we might be throwing the baby out with the bath water. Derek Crispin, in spite of working in the numerate, logical world of financial services, is completely faithful to his own intuitive process:

I'm not comfortable with the all-encompassing word 'intui-tion', but I'm a firm believer in following hunches. I take a Buddhist attitude, which is that your internal being talks to you in a way you shouldn't ignore. A simple example is that if my conscious is suddenly pricked by my speed in the car I *always* slow down. I think of it as fate, as a warning about a potential accident.

Paul Norton does value his intuitive abilities but feels they get squeezed out:

I don't really think I use intuition enough. My role is not well enough defined and I have to wear three different hats: I have to do myself and facilitate in other people research in the forefront of discovery, I have to teach undergraduates, and I have to handle public relations, conferences, budgets and administration. The busyness distracts me from being in-tuitive and I let it slip.

Parminder Sharma is aware of an intensely physical sensation which can give her clues about decisions and judgements:

I use my gut as a sensor, although I may not always acknowledge it. It's a feeling around my tummy. It's like a monitor inside but I do have an element of self-doubt about it. I did, for instance notice this feeling when a subordinate was clearly trying to overtake me on something.

Siobhan felt an intuitive warning of the impending crisis in her last job:

I use my intuition all the time, judge the situation intuitively all the time. I may change a rational prior plan and do things in a different way because of it. In X [her previous job] I began to pick up the vibes; I didn't know what was going on, but I know *something* was. I began to check on things, and record things, and I also decided [in fact she was the subject of a particularly nasty attempt at character assassination] that however nasty other people were I did not intend to be nasty: that way it remained *their* problem.

It is useful to disentangle the 'something-nasty-is-going-on' feeling from paranoia. In fact, I think we slap a 'paranoia' label on a great deal of intuitive material and are often mistaken in doing so. If something makes you uneasy, makes the hair stand up on the back of your neck or does not 'feel right' or 'quite add up', then something nasty *is* going on, although it may not always be completely straightforward to work out what. It is useful to talk material like this over with a trusted friend who understands your line of work but does not work in the same place as you. By expressing your discomfort out loud and hearing it in the outside air you may find it far easier to comprehend what your intuition is trying to tell you.

Link in with your dream life too. Dreams are not composed of transliterable 'symbols' where one thing means another, but they are a rich symbolic medium where feelings can be expressed which may be suppressed during your conscious day. If a dream stays with you the following day, it probably has a message for you. Without straining at making an interpretation, see if a meaning comes into your mind as you reflect on the dream. For example:

> I dreamed I was in a war somewhere and was escaping, in quite a dangerous way. I was running, and at first my eyes were kind of gummed shut. I had to find my way by feeling along the edges of walls, guessing. Eventually they opened, and it was easier to run. My life was at risk, but all the time I was feeling better, knowing I was getting further and further away from the fighting.

This man was considering making a career move. On reflection, being 'in a war' was hardly an obscure symbol for the disturbed state of affairs in the organization he was working for. The dream-story showed an 'escape' when at first he did not know where he was going because his eyes were gummed shut. Escaping from war is obviously a positive move, so the dream is certainly encouraging him to make his change of work.

It seems also to say that it does not matter if at first you are not sure you can 'see where you are going' – just 'feel your way', and your eyes will eventually open spontaneously.

An even simpler dream was this:

> I have been having a perfectly dreadful time with X at work. I dreamed I ripped my fingernails down through her cheek.

This is a bit of aggression which was not expressed during the day. Because it was bottled up, it exploded in a very powerful image. The dream does *not* encourage the dreamer to behave this way in real life – in fact, it probably provides a discharge of emotion which will enable her not to.

If you want to be more in touch with your dream life, keep a notebook by the bed, and write down any dreams you remember on waking. You will retain more dream material this way; otherwise many dreams are elusive and evaporate quickly in the rhythms of everyday routine.

'Listening between the lines' is a skill valued by Angela Winters in her marketing research role. She feels she would not be able to function so successfully if she did not pick up intuitively all the resonances and clues in the language she works with, as well as the literal words. It is interesting to notice a similar point made by a therapist, who says about listening well to clients: 'Never mind the words, listen for the tune.'

David Britton records making a personnel decision recently on the basis of gut feeling. Putting a particular person in charge and making a reorganization has worked out well so far (he says '110 per cent successful') although he sounds a little sheepish about his introspection – 'I'm afraid I depend a lot on what my inner thoughts are telling me.'

Sean McCann is less apologetic and openly says:

> In a lot of my work there's an element of judgement. When you can't rationalize it you rely on 'gut feel'. Much of the decision making I'm involved in you haven't got a set of scales for. I would like to think my 'gut feel' works. I would like to think it has improved.

'Gut feel' or 'intuition' or 'inner thoughts', or even dreams, then, seem to have a great deal to offer in extending the data on which we base our judgements, decisions and actions.

There are challenges and warning notes to consider too,

though Janet King has clear intellectual and ideological objections:

> I am intuitive, but I try *not* to use my intuition. I am a great believer in judgement. I have reservations about 'intuition', because I feel it often feeds a form of prejudice and bigotry. I would *never* take action on the basis of an intuition – I would want to contextualize it and use objective information and criteria.

As Phoebe Driscoll noted, intuition can go wrong. Simon Ayres reveals that his intuition has led him up the garden path several times over the same issue, to the extent that he needs to review why it keeps happening.

> I've been being very generous to someone on the staff because my intuition about her was wrong. It's one of my patterns – to get fooled by strong women who appear weak and vulnerable and then walk all over you. I'm now grovelling to the rest of the staff and apologizing to them because they've carried a can they need not have carried if I had read her right in the first place.

If you become aware that your intuition regularly misfires in one particular area, it is worth taking time to think it over. What pattern in your life is causing you to misread a particular set of signals, and indeed apparently to be drawn back to that misreading to check it over and again? The answer may not be too hard to find. Knowing it will not magically cure the pattern, but the insight may help you survive less scathed, and to make fewer spectacular mistakes because of it.

It may be useful to think of being selective with your intuition to decide when it is appropriate to use it and when it is not.

> I always used to judge people on intuition. I still think you do have to make a quick initial assessment, but I am becoming wary of it. I feel now I ought to check it out afterwards because the intuitive information may be ambiguous and prejudiced.
>
> I'm actually more likely now to trust my instincts about myself. I know I can be creative. I know I can meet my deadlines. (Neil Glover)

Even if you do become selective, events can still conspire to turn your decision on its head:

> I have a tendency to give people the benefit of the doubt. My intuition is against them, but I make my rational side override the intuition. Then they let me down and I wish I hadn't! (Angela Winters)

Developing intuition

We have already spoken of making a good link with your dreams in order to be more aware of subconscious and intuitive messages. Another slight but enjoyable observation you can make is to notice if you are singing a song to yourself, what the words of the song are. We often spontaneously sing songs that are not current or even to our taste, but contain a phrase which is pertinent to our life at the moment. So if you hear yourself singing, 'He's a Real Nowhere Man', or 'It's a Wonderful World', or 'Money, Money, Money', or 'God Only Knows What I'd be Without You' – pause for a moment and see what the message is that you are telling yourself.

Every personal interaction however apparently superficial has its own physiology. Pupils dilate or contract, hormones are increased in the bloodstream, the sweat intensifies or disintensifies in pheramone content. Vasodilation in the face and throat increases or decreases, the body relaxes or tenses, the breathing quickens or slows. All of that information is assimilated. I think one's intuition in terms of being able to predict how successful a working relationship is going to be, whether it is truth or lies that is being told, whether a person's energies are well enough aligned to do a good job for you, can be improved by learning to be aware of all those things, and how to read them in the way that works for you. I feel doubtful that this-equals-that tricksy interpretations of these inter-personal physiologies can be a great deal more useful than this-equals-that 'dictionaries' of dream symbols. It seems to me to be much more likely that building up a database of calm self-observation will help you to interpret your 'gut feel' reactions to people and situations in a way that is useful and constructive for you.

Any bodywork that you do will enhance your ability to do this, because it will increase your physical and physiological sensibilities. It may seem strange to think that running, or dance class, or any other physical training can help build your intuition in the professional field, but it undoubtedly can, because it will deepen your ability to 'read' your own body. Non-exercisers need not despair because any constructive and co-ordinated physical activity that is done with real energy will do the same thing. You do not have to be doing circuit training to achieve this: you could just as well be walking, or gardening, or making love.

Finally, not dismissing your intuitions, but noticing them, reviewing whether they were correct and whether they were useful, which issues you seem to be perceptive about and where you seem to draw blanks, will little by little grow your intuitive faculty into a useful contributory factor in your life. Do not write intuition off because management is supposed to be a macho activity, and intuition has always been characterized as a feminine skill.

TRIGGER FOUR:
Do you ever use intuition at work? If you do, what happens?

Communication out

Once we start valuing gut feelings in ourselves, we start respecting gut feelings in other people too. Opening up the best possible channel of communication is all we can do. Not everybody will have a positive gut feeling about you; but it is a pity if someone, be they colleague or client, builds up a negative gut feeling just because of poor communications. It is not always possible to be completely open because information is a highly strategic commodity, and also because you may find it useful to work out how much or how little of yourself you wish to make public at work. The aim, nevertheless, within your chosen boundaries, could be to be clear.

Assertiveness

Assertive communication is invaluable for clarifying 'communication out'. It is based on an inner equilibrium characterized by neither a 'power over' nor an over-powered one, but a sense of *power within.*

With a clear sense of your own 'power within', you can begin to use the 'core phrase' technique. This is a method of condensing what you need to say into a clear, concise 'core phrase'. With practice you can eliminate apologetic or diversionary 'padding', and simply be clear. The core phrase can be reiterated as often as necessary to get your message across and has the advantage of sounding not aggressive but firm, not inflexible but clear and not idiosyncratic but balanced.

A marvellous quality of assertiveness is that it works well to disidentify the messenger from the message, the person from the idea, the criticizer from the criticism, when those identifications can become disruptive. We are familiar, from the world of (national) politics, how issues can become confused with personalities, and liking someone (or their TV and media persona) can get confused with agreeing with their ideas. The same blurring can happen with policy issues in any organizations and it is a great advantage to be able to avoid it.

An assertive mode is also useful in conveying both good and bad news in a clear and calm manner, and in giving positive and negative feedback without entangling inappropriate emotions. It helps you to stand your ground without getting tense if that is what you need to do; and conversely, if you have to back down on a matter, or acknowledge a mistake, it does help you to do so without rolling in the dirt.

Communicating assertively can relieve one of the compulsion to be liked by everybody. It is a great liberation to feel that one is not hurt by another person's candid dislike, and to notice that one can, oddly, often work very effectively with a person where the dislike between the two of you is well ventilated and not taken personally on either side. (The technique is fully discussed in *Positive Management Assertiveness for Managers*, Paddy O'Brien, Brealey, 1992.)

Boundaries

It is useful to get clear about where your boundaries are; and to give yourself some specific time to work that out. You may be prepared to speak about all, some, or no areas of your private life in the workplace, and you may be prepared to receive confidences or have conversations about some, all or none of the personal issues for your staff in their private lives. You can be clear without being aggressive about what you feel is appropriate, and what you feel is not. The advantage of thinking this through is that you do not get drawn into sharing something which afterwards you wish you had not shared, or hearing something which afterwards you wish you had not heard.

The same internal/external negotiations apply while getting clear how much work-socializing and work-travelling you want to or have to get involved in. Organizational cultures vary enormously on how much or how little they expect from you in these areas, but you can be active rather than passive in making a positive choice about where to pitch yourself in their expectations.

Body language and voice quality

The words we hear from a person's mouth are only a small proportion of the total message we take in (some behavioural psychologists estimate it at around thirty per cent). The rest of the message comes from body language, and voice pitch, tone and pace.

Again, give yourself time to make active rather than passive choices about your body language and your voice usage within the context of your organization. Decide where to pitch yourself in the organizational dress code. Tiny adjustments can establish your belief in your own creativity or capability, without overwhelming anybody else. Lengthening the spine and loosening the joints results in a relaxed, alert body state which is confident without being aggressive. Steady breathing calms not only you but the people around you as well.

Listen to the vocal range used in your place of work: in a

creative/media environment people may talk fastish and in the upper range, whereas in a financial management environment, rather fast, harsh low tones are favoured. A meeting of medical consultants speaks in the middle range and with enormous assurance, where the mellifluous, concerned, low-pitched tones of those (like myself!) in advisory/consultancy roles concerning stress and violence management and developmental issues are easy to recognize. These are all specific examples I have noticed and are not intended to be generalizations: however, if you take a day or two to observe it, you will see that a particular style of discourse prevails in your workplace, or maybe several different ones if there are several sub-groups. It is a very powerful thing to do to make positive, active choices about how much of that style to take into yourself and how much to be different, rather than passively to be sucked into organizationspeak. It may give you a cosy sense of belonging at first, but will erode your personal power and decisiveness in the long run.

3. **Mine's bigger than yours**

There is a problem with owning a lot. There is a problem with getting more and more.

The more you have, and the more you get, the more you have to look after. The more you might lose. Is that owning or being owned?

(John Heider: *The Tao of Leadership*)

What does the macho manager do about the status game? And what does the manager who is thinking about reviewing the macho ethos do about the status game? Is it escapable or is it inevitable? And if it is escapable do we want to escape, and finally, if we do want to escape, how are we going to do so?

We can begin by standing back and noticing what the status symbols in our particular line of work might be. Think of your own colleagues, your own workplace. What possessions and what activities invoke all the emotions that attach to status: envy, jealousy, pride, anxiety, longing? Make a list and add to it as things occur to you.

Let us look first at that most potent symbol of 'mine's bigger than yours' – the internal combustion engine. It will be fascinating to see what happens during the next decade to the company car. The car fulfils a number of semiological functions and structural economic functions which make it ideal as a status symbol. It is easy in many jobs to create a rationale where the car is necessary for the travelling involved in the job itself; so it has an apparently clear function. It also has a clear functional value as a perk – providing an employee with a good efficient car and picking up the bill for repairs is a tax-efficient way of giving them the equivalent of several thousand extra pounds of income a year. However, apart from that, a car is like something you wear, it says a great deal about the value the company places on you; the choice you make within the available band of cars says a great deal about your own confidence and self-image. Not only that, a car is bigger than you physically, and highly visible: a Rolex watch may be very expensive, but it cannot show up as much as a car, and you cannot drive it! The concept of a car's 'performance' is so strongly linked in the subconscious mind with sexual performance that a large fast car with powerful acceleration is a loud and obvious message about the driver's virility, both literally and in the business context. So, a car works very well as a message which says: my company values me, *I* value me, I am successful, proactive, thrusting, virile. So far, so good. It is a divisive force, it is an envy-creating enterprise, part of a process designed to foster aspiration and ambition. Pay is supposed to be confidential and usually is but cars are a code which tells everyone in a public way what you earn. It slots you into a pecking order even though everyone is pretending that there is not one.

Two important problems emerge, however. One is: what about women? The second is: what about the planet? Let us look at women first – or perhaps we should say womanliness, or, perhaps we should broaden it further and say *yin* qualities. If the most prevalent status symbol used in the corporate reward system is a symbol of phallic puissance, what does that say about how much that company's culture values narrow 'masculine behaviour', and what does it say to the women that company employs, and further, what does it say to the men and women in that company who value their 'yin' abilities as well as their 'yang' ones?

Women who drive powerful cars evoke a confused response from both women and men. The initial assumption is that the car must belong to a man with whom she is connected – a boss, a husband, a boyfriend, a father. If it becomes clear that the car belongs to the woman herself the reaction is a combination of awe, envy and fear. This reaction sets in at a much 'lower' grade of car possessed by women than it does by men: i.e. people might feel that combination of reactions to a male Rolls Royce owner, but they will feel them about a female BMW owner. Should a woman run and own a sports car, she will find herself creating an even more acute stir. Again, the first assumption will be that someone else gave her the car. Because a sports car has a heightened sexual image, it will be assumed that she is a mistress rather than a wife. If it becomes clear that it is her own car, it will be assumed that she is an astonishing package of slag/sex kitten/exhibitionist, and also that she is wildly over-compensating for unrequited nymphomania by owning such a machine. I know because I owned one once: a rather mild sort of sports car, which my brother fulfilled his macho needs with by hurling it around the country until it was nearly clapped out, at which point he gave it to me. (I see, by the way, that this puts me into the category of being given a car by a man.) I enjoyed the way people got out of my way in the fast lane because they assumed from the car's silhouette that it would be travelling at terrific speed. I found the other reactions, the assumptions about my attitudes, more confusing to deal with. There are some cars which, as a culture, we are all quite comfortable with women owning – nippy little Renaults, slick little Micras, white cars, red cars, smart and sleek, with semiological links with products like powder compacts (shiny, snappy) or other 'fun' products (zany, whacky, vivacious). Serious, fast, heavy cars, are not congruent with women and womanliness at all.

Thus, a woman who works in a company where getting a big car is a significant rite of passage, has a complicated package of messages and consequences to cope with. So too does a man who sees himself as 'yin' as well as 'yang', as having 'more to him' than exclusively the 'macho' range of qualities.

What strategies might be useful for dealing with this? Initially, when women began to make an impact in senior tiers of management, it seemed to be important simply to get hold of the status symbols, including the big car, and to demonstrate being a woman in possession of those status symbols.

This begs the crucial question: do you buy *into* the *status quo*, or do you buy *out* of it? Do you take on the values of the environment you work in, or do you keep these at arm's length, and have your own value system? If your values are different from prevailing cultural values, do you keep that secret, or show the difference in an unchallenging way, or show the difference in a way that challenges and seeks to influence the *status quo*? If women want to be in senior management, how much must they take on 'macho' values as protective colouring or as practical *modus vivendi*? If men want to be in senior management must they suppress their 'female' qualities for purposes of protective colouring or as a practical *modus vivendi*?

It seems possible that now is the time to detach yourself from that value system if you want to, and if you feel very attracted to big fast cars as rewards, at least to review that in the light of what those big fast cars *mean*.

Let us come now to our second question – what about the planet? As we have said, we can usefully look at our attitudes to the company car in the light of gender issues and 'macho' issues. Post-Rio, nobody can be ignorant about the consequences of big, fast, and numerous cars on the environment. It has taken twenty years for this thinking to move from an agenda labelled 'lunatic fringe', to an agenda which international governments know they must address. Somehow we have to integrate our personal and insular needs and desires with the imperative of slowing down our damage to the environment.

The fiscal position on company cars has recently, in some ways, reflected this. From Nigel Lawson's 1988 budget onwards, taxation on company fleets has been high. The 1992 budget made a significant cut in car tax, which was a relaxation of pressure on the company car situation, but also introduced a National Insurance charge on company cars payable by employers, which put pressure on. Of course one can feel cynical about successive governments joyfully embracing the environmental message because it gives them an ideologically respectable excuse to hike up their tax revenue. Even so, however pure or muddy the motives, the signs are that the tax position on company cars will reflect the increasing pressure of environmental awareness.

A growth in individual awareness of the consequences of running a car, of the importance of the way cars are used (fully or empty, short or long trips, catalytic convertor or not, unleaded petrol or not) may drain away our desire to project so much magic into our travelling machines. Should we (faint hope) be blessed with a government which develops an integrated, pollution-sensitive transport policy, the need for little individual tin boxes (however stylish) will be much diminished anyway.

If, for these reasons, big fast cars during the next decade cease to be the vehicle (in every sense) of so much mystique and charisma, it will be intriguing to see where all that material gets displaced. It will be equally fascinating to see whether any significant status symbol which takes the car's place will be another macho metaphor, or a more yin/yang balanced item.

Gadgets, clothes and people

The filofax was the essential accessory of the eighties – its subtext:

> I'm so fantastically busy I have to have everything noted in here, my network is so huge I have to have notes of it all in here. I am so creative and quick thinking that my torrent of ideas has to be noted on the hundreds of little stickers sticking out of the pages.

In the early nineties the little personal computer notebooks have taken their place. Notes are tapped, stored, analysed and coded in these, which say, 'I'm at ease with the technology, I or my company can easily afford one of these, and I don't store anything on paper these days.'

Do you have one? Do you want one? What does it or would it do for you? What does it do to you if somebody else has one and you do not?

What about clothes as status symbols? Many men manage to screen out their awareness of how other men dress, and thus immunize themselves from power games around male dressing, although some are aware of the confidence-giving and confidence-taking properties of better-cut jackets, better quality cloth, more exciting neckties, more expensive overcoats, supple and expensive shoes. Neither women nor men are immune to significant status-dressing among women, the telegraphy of confidence and competence made by expensive tailoring and a colour range not available in cheap clothing. Women sometimes 'play' with macho/feminine combinations by, for example, wearing severely tailored suits with transparent blouses and transparent underwear underneath. Although this is an 'interesting' contrast – and with AIDS and sex crime being pressing realities in the nineties, many fashion 'statements' involve a sexual come-on garment combined with a turn-off item, for instance the way very young women wear gauzy skirts with heavy Doc Martins or trainers – women do need to think through what the consequences of giving such a mixed message may be. Women may strongly feel that men use their sexuality freely at work – to bond with other men, to manipulate and/or exclude women, to exercise power – so why should women not use their own sexuality as a source of power? I do not think there is an easy answer to this, but it does seem clear that using the male definition of female sexuality as a means of claiming power is colluding with the macho model of behaviour rather than innovating by stepping away from it. If the workplace was less underpinned by macho values, there would be less pressure on this area altogether.

The space you get in the office speaks of your status too. Do you get a desk by the window, an office of your own, if so, how big is it? Does it have plants, pictures, a secretary? In straitened times, secretaries take on totemic value during staff cuts.

> Somebody's secretary had to go, [says Sean McCann] but it wasn't going to be *mine*. It became a power thing among the five of us, who was going to be forced to let their secretary go. It had to do with whose work had the least and whose the most status, and therefore had greatest claim to be got out of the door most quickly.

A (usually female) secretary may be a status symbol of one kind, and a 'trophy wife' may be a status symbol of a similar but distinguishable sort. A man who has become highly successful, highly accessorized with prestige products, may deliberately or unconsciously trade in his middle-aged wife for a younger, sleeker person, who fits the 'image' and the 'life-style' of the successful executive better. No doubt few of these partnerships are contracted in this completely heartless way, but the predisposition to behave thus is inherent in the macho culture where young attractive women are almost another 'consumer item' which demonstrates the power and status of their 'owner'. While a mix of young, beautiful people, and old beautiful people, and young plain people, and old plain people, should naturally all be part of any workforce, an awful lot hangs on who defines beauty, what the definition of beauty is, how being beautiful links in with power and status in that workplace (for instance, do you have to *be* it if you are female, and *own* it or control it if you are male?), to determine whether what is happening is fair or not. It probably is not: and it probably is not fair, in the final analysis, to either sex. To take just a few examples:

> I think X is more efficient than Y (both women), although I always thought Y was quite sexy. Lots of the people in the office fancied her. (Male manager 1991)

> We did have a situation where the choice was between two equal women. We did choose on the basis of who was most attractive. (Male manager 1992)

Of course there is a physiological component, which may include sexual attraction, in any interaction between any two people of whatever sex. No one denies that. What matters is what significance that is given, what language it is expressed in, and what power relationships arise as a result of it.

> He should have taken X on that trip with him. She was the appropriate person to go. She would have been brilliant. But he couldn't because his wife couldn't cope with it. It was so unfair on X, it makes me so angry. (One male manager, referring to another, 1990)

If sex and power were not habitually reckoned on a macho basis in the workplace, maybe the mythology would not have been in place to make the man's wife feel threatened, so that she would not feel unhappy about the trip, X need not have missed the opportunity, and the man need not have had the pressure and disadvantage of having to make the trip without his best member of staff.

Gay and lesbian people have an additional complication to cope with in the sex/status tangle in the workplace. If they do not disclose their homosexuality they will be expected to play the macho games, speak the language, and display the 'appropriate' reactions, which is highly stressful and compromising. They will

also hear all the unrestrained homophobic language and senti-
ment that is a corollary to these. If they are out, they may be
exhausted by having to 'represent' gay opinion and make
assertive responses to the habitual anti-gay language and behaviour around them. Some professions are more gay-friendly
and accustomed to integrating gays than others, and some have a
strong ideological commitment to a prejudice-free work place,
while others are still deeply and paranoically homophobic.
However far down the Equal Opportunities road an organization
has gone though, this remains essentially a heterosexual and
heterosexist culture, so there is always extra and different work
for gay people to do around status, sex and power.

Access

> Flacks were wearing their summit press-credential necklace
> everywhere too – not tucking them in a pocket as usual, but
> letting all the little plastic cards hang outside their Burberrys like
> kindergarteners sent home with notes to mother pinned on their
> snowsuits.

(P. J. O'Rourke, *Holidays in Hell*, Pan, 1989)

Are there areas of access in your profession or in your particular
office which have glamour, power and status attached to them?
Who gets invited to launches and seminars, who has the media
contact and the media profile, who gets wined and dined and
entertained, or invited to speak or publish or join steering
committees? Think through the ways in which access to contacts,
invitations and opportunities can create differences and imbalances in what Peter Middleton calls the 'ghostly pecking
order'. If someone makes a display of their accesses, as they did in
O'Rourke's example of journalists at a significant political
summit displaying their ID tags, how does that make you feel? If
you have a much prized invitation or 'insider' ticket of some
kind, do you make sure everybody sees it? O'Rourke has a huge
contempt for anyone in his profession who tries to aggrandize
themselves because of important things happening around them:

Some writers, the young and the dim ones, think being near something important makes them important so they should act and sound important which will, somehow, make their audience important, too. Then, as soon as everybody is filled with a sufficient sense of importance, Something Will Be Done. It's not the truth. Thirty years of acting and sounding important about the Holocaust did nothing to prevent Cambodia. (O'Rourke, op. cit.)

The macho trap here is to go for everything and be exhibitionist about what you acquire in the way of access and invitations. There is a core of useful promotional activity which gets turned into a status game. What we need to do to get a balanced line on it is to explore the possibilities on their merits and decide what is really worth attending and putting energy into.

This is useful because it avoids frittering time away at endless marginally developmental receptions and functions, and it preserves a certain cachet because it is clear you are being selective when you do attend. It is useful to work out how this dynamic operates in your office or place of work, and how you want to place yourself within it.

Formal appraisal systems

TRIGGER FIVE:

How is good performance measured in your organization? How is it rewarded?

All the status issues we have discussed are part of the performance-reward system in an organization. Some, like cars, may be awarded in a structured way. Others come more haphazardly through grace and favour with little reference to fairness.

Many organizations now have put or are putting a formal appraisal system in place. Targets and achievements have to be clearly defined and measured, so that the BS 5750 or IS 9000 criteria can be met. Increasingly organizational self-knowledge, thoughtful policy-making and clear forward planning are required by funders of all kinds to a degree unheard of even ten years ago, and formulating a clear appraisal system is a key

element in this. Is there an appraisal system available for you?
David Britton wishes there was:

> This is a very unstructured company with regard to
> appraisals. I think we work on the assumption that if you're
> doing a good job you keep your job, and if you aren't you lose
> it. No one tells me if I'm doing a good or a bad job and really I
> would welcome it if they did. There is a bonus system but
> there doesn't seem to be any clear-cut logic to it, it doesn't bear
> much relationship to results.

This is hardly the caring company of the nineties, and takes a
pretty macho line; the implicit message is: 'If we don't sack you
you can assume you're doing OK.'

It may be frustrating not to have an appraisal system at all, but
it may be even worse to have a bad one. Janet King finds the
appraisal system at her place of work:

> deplorable. It is pay-related, it is badly done, I believe it is in
> breach of the Equal Opportunities legislation. It is not given
> proper time, it is not given proper training, it is not a forum
> for improvement. I have said all this quite publicly.

Janet feels angry because the appraisal system she has to contend
with is poorly designed, not underpinned by preparation and
training, and is a thoroughly wasted opportunity for exchange
and development.

One stage worse than this is when the appraisal system actually
gets abused. Sean McCann says:

> Theoretically our performance is measured by an appraisal
> system. It is poorly used by the appraisees who you might
> think would have an interest in using it well. The appraisers
> use it in a corrupt way. They make gut feel judgements and
> then write reports to fit them.

The dissatisfactions of these two give us an interesting clue to
what the key elements of a *good* formal appraisal system should
be. By reflecting back the opposites of what they report as their
experience we can see that we need a workable and constructive
appraisal system to be –

- *open*: that is, without hidden agendas, with provision for clear access to information, and clear criteria on which assessments are made.

- *confidential*: so that it is agreed in advance who has access to information and who does not.

- *creative and developmental*: in order for the outcome of the review to encourage the person to develop *and the organization to develop*.

- *participative*: both the appraiser and the appraisee should be part of the system.

- *consistent*: criteria should be agreed and applied evenly.

- *monitorable*: it must be possible to check that objectives are being met.

- *accountable*: the system must be accountable to the organization, the appraiser and the appraisee.

- *resourced*: time and training must be adequate both for appraisers and appraisees.

- *simple*: attempts to be fair can produce an undesirably baroque structure to your appraisal system. It is well worth the investment of time to simplify it as much as possible.

Siobhan Boyle finds it strange to work presently in a unit where there are no appraisal structures at all, after coming from a place with a complex scheme:

> We are not measured at all here. Zilch. We have a new female Chief Executive who is trying to bring it all together – before her there were simply warring factions, and we are still bogged down in separate units. There is nothing here, you just move up the payscale on the basis of passage of time. Where I used to work the appraisal scheme was mutual and useful, so long as you trusted the person you were dealing with.

Phoebe Driscoll operates within an appraisal system which is practical, workable, and appropriate for the aims of her organization:

We are performance driven and we are budget driven. Staff are paid on a layered commission system by numbers generated and by income generated, but they are also assessed by their quality of service and their interaction with colleagues, so you can't have someone who is hell to work with and disrupts other colleagues shooting to the top.

The very formality of a good appraisal system is part of its strength; many people emphasize the importance of a 'public ritual', particularly of celebration of achievements and projects well performed. If there are questions of adjustments and improvements to be made by staff, the structured approach of a good appraisal scheme creates a space in which this can happen without subjectivity and emotion.

A further benefit of an appraisal system which is functioning well is the accuracy of attribution that arises from it. If things are going well, you need to know why, and if things are going badly you need to know why that is too. The discussions that arise in an appraisal session can be used to focus those, to sharpen up analysis and clear up erroneous assumptions. When you have got correct attribution for both your good results and your bad results, you can do much more informed planning.

Informal reward systems

Janet King creates in her working environment a complete contrast to David Britton's 'no-celebration' culture.

In my *department* [as opposed to the 'deplorable' overall system] we assert that line management is a *right*. A fixed person will always give a staff member time and space. There are comprehensive reviews with documentation, discussion and follow-ups, goals and targets are set for the following year and a three-yearly plan is made, which is all fully documented and reviewed. It is important *always* to tell people when things are good. I have a huge selection of postcards which I send out at the rate of five or six a week to congratulate people on specific pieces of good work. They are known as 'Janet's cards'! I sent one the other day, for example, to a Special

Needs Inspector of mine who did a really good display. I take in wine or small presents and say publicly when things are going well, and if it's significant enough to warrant it I drop a formal note in the file.

I'm not necessarily easy, and I never let anything go that is incompetent, but I do look for a strategy to address mistakes, I wouldn't just dump on them.

People who now want to work for Janet are advised to form an orderly queue, as indeed they do within her own organization.

Janet has an exceptionally developed sense both of the importance of feedback and of the most effective ways of giving it. She avoids becoming a kind of dominatrix, however benevolent, by combining all this with a real awareness of team competence, team development, and regular team exercises where she hears feedback from her staff as well as the other way around.

Somewhat more gloomily, Paul Norton sees an informal reward-system in his place of work which reflects what he calls the 'ghostly pecking order' – where, for example, 'you get a bigger office purely for time-serving'.

An informal reward-system, to work well, has to have all the hallmarks of a successful formal appraisal system. It has to be consistent, transparent (no hidden agendas) and open (no secrets), or it can be divisive, perceived as an abuse of power, or an expression of an individual manager's moods and whims. It has to be backed up by times when the feedback can flow the other way, or it does become unbalanced. If it fulfils these criteria though, it can be a powerful energizer of staff and a powerful bonding agent for a working team.

Personal rewards

TRIGGER SIX:

What kind of rewards do you aspire to most at the moment?

Money

We may envy the few people we know who love their work so

much that money is really of no relevance to them. The reality for the vast majority of us is quite different and money is a key index of our achievement. That is why we are prepared to fight quite hard for the salary we feel we deserve.

This is also why we see in other people and may sense in ourselves the capacity to sacrifice too much for the cause of money. What kind of rewards really please and motivate you? Do you want to be taken out for an expensive meal? Do you want a Porsche, or an expensive coat, or a holiday somewhere exotic? Or do you seek rewards of a different kind, such as recognition of your efforts by colleagues and bosses, or a sense that what you do actually matters to somebody somewhere, or a knowledge that through your own work your own opportunities and life are enhanced and transformed? Do you have a particular and specific desire to express yourself, or assert yourself? It is worth pausing to analyse this question for yourself because in a hectic life it is all too easy to lose sight of the 'why' because you are giving all your energy to the 'what' the 'when' the 'where' and the 'how'. You may work your guts out so as to get more money so as to buy more things, so you need more money in order to buy yet more things, and so forth. We have unexamined assumptions about our life-styles, about what sort of equipment we need, what sort of kit we need, what sort of treats we need. The useful thing about pausing to examine those assumptions is to re-evaluate that your rewards really do make you feel good and your require-ments really are what you think they are.

Neil Glover feels instant affirmation when he is paid:

> I enjoy the moment the cheque comes through the door. I see the money as concrete recognition of my work.

Angela Winters has a sense of changing from a desire for abstract to a need for more solid symbols of recognition.

> I used to be satisfied by sheer interest in what I do. I don't know if it's cynicism or what but now I'm looking for more tangible financial rewards.

On the other hand, with some provisos, the shift for Julia Primera has been in the other direction:

Early on in my career I wanted organizational recognition, promotion in my specialism, status, money. Now I want more a feeling of having made a difference, of having touched people in a way that makes a difference. I do want money, but I want it for the freedom it buys me, which is access to child care, being able to buy good quality clothes. It gives me some kind of status and dignity – if I'm out there earning this kind of money. I have status, I have a role. I don't have to ask for money from my partner or justify to him what I spend it on. It gives me independence.

This is a very money-based culture. The ability to generate substantial amounts of money tends to enhance our sense of self, and gaps and dips in earning power can erode our sense of self badly. Sometimes it seems that only people who have been high earners have the freedom to 'come out the other side' and drop the pursuit of wealth as a central goal; but it is useful to all of us, whatever our financial status at the moment, to become aware of how this is functioning for us, particularly in management when we are making decisions about just how far up the ladder to push. Women have always had practice with this because of the experiences, like those hinted at by Julia Primera, that they have coped with during career breaks while having children. With the chronic instability of employment patterns in the nineties any of us may face a sudden career break any time, and face the consequent loss of earnings and loss of power and identity.

Generating sufficient money to provide food, shelter and the basics of life for ourselves and our dependants is one thing. Generating extra money for enjoyment is another. This blurs into a third, which is generating money for items which display our ability to generate money.

Loss of earning power is often described in terms of male castration – men and women are heard to describe themselves as 'emasculated' by being unable to generate enough money for that first category, that is, of basic necessities. With both the economy and the welfare state in dire straits more of us will undergo a crisis of this sort in the next decade than ever before. The second and third categories, with their sometimes shifting boundary, fulfil a need to be 'effective' in a masculine sense too, and an inability to do so gives a similar, if less drastic, sense of emasculation. It would be whimsical to suggest that we can insure ourselves against such feelings of vulnerability by working out that it is 'macho' and deciding not to be. It may, however, be useful, to notice that certainly the third, and arguably the second of those money-generating capabilities (money for status symbols, and money for fun), is an aspect of validation being given from the outside, and not from within, as would be the darker, more inner and reflective yin or feminine response.

Many women and men become irritated by the predictable pop-psychology analysis of our heartache. 'Low self-esteem', they say. 'Of course', we snap, annoyed at the glibness, despairing about the inevitability. 'Low self-esteem' is an *epidemic* among women. On short reflection it is not difficult to work out why: the mixed messages every little girl gets about her intelligence, her appearance, her ambitions, her achievements, her attitude. The contradictions that are set up before she reaches puberty are enough to set up the potential for a lifetime's low self-esteem for most women. Any woman who manages to bring her self-esteem into a calm and positive equilibrium is a heroine and role-model as far as I am concerned.

On further examination, though, we can see that 'low self-esteem' or at least 'precarious self-esteem' is a strong ingredient in many men's lives too. Paul Norton, who has studied masculinity and male self-imaging, says:

> Culture sets up manhood as an ideal achieved through competition. This is ingrained in the narratives of the stories little boys read in comics and see through the media.

Men can feel quite daunted by those images. If you have got to succeed competitively to 'achieve manhood', you are going to worry about failing competitively, and lots of men do worry precisely about this. The money-status game becomes particularly pressing, to show you *are* succeeding in that 'manhood competition'. Any man who has freed or partly freed himself from that pressure is equally inspiring.

Take time to think through your own relationship with:

- money for necessities
- money for fun
- money for status-symbols
- money as an index of your personal value

See whether there are any surprises and any points that you would like to change. If there are changes, think specifically about how you will begin to put them in train.

Reputation

'I want to be well thought of', says Simon Ayres. This is followed by a spurt of self contempt: 'I suppose I want to be the "little friend of all the world" '. Managers in and out of the so-called 'caring professions' will recognize his impulse.

Chris Hargreaves says:

> I want recognition both in the council and beyond as someone who is successful, innovative, and good at implementing change.

He is clear that he wants a profile not just in his own organization, but carrying out to the world outside it too: perhaps with a view to future promotion or office, but perhaps as an important piece of personal fulfilment too.

Cara Frances's environment is the publishing industry, and she says:

> There is incredibly intense grapevining. It is amazing given that business is apparently conducted in formal meetings but messages exchanged in the corridor or the loo are much more powerful. Personnel move rapidly from firm to firm and interlinks are formed that way too. Your personal reputation is extremely important

Derek Crispin knows what an important reward unequivocal praise can be:

> Whenever a member of my staff does something well, they get effusive praise from me. I firmly believe in credit where credit's due. . . . My ways of rewarding people are a) to give

them greater responsibility, b) to give them a pat on the back, and c) to give them a financial reward; but I know that the pat on the back is like gold, often worth *more* than money.

He adds thoughtfully:

You've got to respect the person it's coming from. Praise is not worth a lot if there is little respect across the board.

Forming and developing a good reputation in that context is a necessity for professional survival, but is also a factor for personal reward. It is, of course, very gratifying if colleagues who understand your job from the inside, admire your work and give you positive feedback in a generous way. It is very pleasant and nourishing if senior staff give you good feedback too, although in all but the most transparent and committed developmental organizations, there are inevitably political and self protective elements in any such discourse. It is crucial however to balance the public, interactive, yang side of 'having a good reputation' with the inner yin side of thinking well of yourself, being a clear and calm assessor of your own performance. In the last analysis, anyone who can give you approval, can also take it away again. You need to have your internal affairs arranged so that you do not fall flat on your face if that happens.

Think through whose opinions you value and how praise from them makes you feel. Think through the ways you criticize yourself and the times you think well of yourself, and how those factors make you feel. Notice any patterns. Question seriously praise *or* blame which upsets your equilibrium, and see if you can sense what you need to do to receive the nurturing and developmental positive feedback you need without becoming dependent on anybody else. This may change your perspective about many things.

Joan Yates is one of the very few women in a senior role in her field. The aura around her is calm, and the sense of achievement in her new appointment is not of a person who gets there with a heap of corpses under her feet, but a person who is fruitfully fulfilling her own potential. 'Self-satisfaction' is normally a phrase with negative connotations and so is 'being pleased with oneself', but I feel we hear very positive self-satisfaction, and an example of high-level attainment without a macho attitude in Joan's remarks here:

> I'm very happy. I've just been promoted to a job I've been working towards for five years. I'm very happy with that recognition and now I want to consolidate everything both professionally and personally.

Think through what would have to happen in your life for effort and reward to meet each other in a synthesis like this. Once you can see this clearly you have a sense of what would be a good match of blood, sweat and tears with pay and status for you, without getting side-tracked in ways you do not want to be in the status game. Once you have done that, you can see the goal. All you have to do after that is draw the map and find the way!

4. **Survival of the fittest**

The journey of the soul is so difficult that the body needs to be very strong to carry the soul through it. Have you ever thought of it that way round? That is to say, that your spiritual/intellectual journey can, in this world at least, only be made within the vehicle of your body and that journey is so strenuous that you have to make your physical self tough to withstand it. This is Yoga thinking, this is the reason why as well as meditative and reflective practice, Yoga espouses a set of exercises which, when you get to grips with them, are not a series of gentle little stretches, but profoundly expansive and athletic exercises to make the body a brave and resilient soul-carrier.

Managers, on the whole, get rewarded for their head-work. Good thinking, good manoeuvring, taking initiatives, fighting for opportunities and repelling threats are recognized and rewarded as worthy activities. Few companies, if any, give brownie points for physical strength and well-being. The risk is that we start using our bodies simply as machines for carrying our heads around on.

It may well be useful to re-connect the strength of the body and the strength and resilience of the mind, and to look at how the two can work together for us as managers. Companies and employing institutions may not attend to good health but they do attend to the breakdown of health – absences for sickness are an important part of any personnel record. In exactly the way that our National Health Service (what remains of it) has become a national sickness service, organizations may find detox facilities (though probably only for senior staff) but not address the reasons for addiction in the first place. This 'macho' position on health is echoed by the individuals in a macho culture, who also attend to it only when it becomes sickness:

I rarely think about my health except when I'm ill. I've had some bad moments recently. I get odd frights like horrendous midnight coughs and chest tightening, which reminds me how much I smoke [forty a day]. I'm probably doing my body a lot of long-term damage but because there are no direct symptoms I'm keeping it under wraps. (Sean McCann)

This interesting reflection is almost steretypically 'macho' – the assumption that non-awareness of the body is the norm, and that signals from the body are anomalous – 'odd frights'. He also counters a feeling that he may be doing 'long-term damage' with the surprising assertion that there are 'no direct symptoms' even though he has just explained that he wakes up in the night with a choking cough. He knows, in fact, that he is becoming ill, but as considering this thoughtfully is unacceptable in his cultue, he will have to reach a crisis of some kind before he can allow himself to take it seriously. Some women find that the endless task of managing periods, fertility, pregnancy and the menopause, allows them to form a relationship with and sensitivity to their bodies which can develop into the resilience and strength to survive their managerial role well. Women among themselves do not, in general, regard it as a weakness to swap news, informa-tion, and opinions about their health, both uterine and otherwise. However, women committed to success at work are under pressure to avoid being seen to be involved in anything that could be construed as 'women's talk', or indeed to display anything that could be called 'women's troubles'. That would be seen as diminishing.

Men have recently 'come out of the closet' about prostate problems: the condition itself, its effects and treatments. This sharing begins to provide a welcome balance in accepting the vulnerability of the human body, of whichever gender. The stress this creates is discussed below in the section 'Life cycles'. Working to eclipse their female body-cycles, rather than to ride them or flow with them in a powerful way – working, indeed, to emulate Sean McCann's behaviour and 'keep it under wraps', some high-flying women fall into a frustrating and upsetting pattern of allergies and viral infections which are elusive to diagnose and to treat.

Let us look at our own attitudes to our own bodies in sickness and in health, in youth and in ageing, in exhaustion, addiction, and also in well-being, and consider how it would feel to shift our perspective in such a way that maintaining and sustaining our bodies became part of our calm success-planning – making the body a strong and resilient vehicle for the career you want to have and the life you want to lead. Begin with this trigger:

TRIGGER SEVEN:
How would you describe your state of health at the moment? What are you most pleased about with regard to your health? And what are you least pleased about?

We could collect and focus our thoughts by considering some of the elements which make up our health – our health-profile or health-picture: food, sleep, exercise, life-cycles, anxiety and well-being. This is not a definitive list nor are the components always clearly separable, but it is a useful way of getting thoughts and reactions to flow.

Food

One government information campaign after another exhorts us to eat in a more healthy fashion, to be aware of the impact of diet on avoiding heart attacks, and so forth. Their cohorts have little chance against the enormous publicity budgets of the food industry, which fill TV advertising slots with messages about an extraordinary array of, in the main, 'unhealthy' highly processed foods. Anyone who has travelled recently in France will be interested to notice the lack of food advertising combined with the universal availability of lovely food. It is a culture where almost no energy goes into trying to make any foodstuff look or sound nicer than it actually is, and yet it is almost impossible to get nasty food at all.

Men and women tend to have different preoccupations about food, with men prioritizing appeal and quantity, and women desperately trying to find 'healthy' and low-calorie options.

You may have a deep enjoyment of tastes and textures of food, of companionable ('con-pane' is 'taking bread together') times, or you may be aware chiefly of how any excess calories you take in will glue themselves relentlessly to your hips and thighs. It all depends what is happening for you when you are eating. If you can begin to understand that, you can begin to get hold of what is driving your eating patterns, their balances and imbalances, their pleasures and pains: and if you can understand those, there is a good chance that you can make any adjustments you want to, which will help you to keep your body well and strong in a calm and balanced way.

Too much

> I very much regret that I am overweight at the moment. (Mark Ellis)

> I overindulge in food and in drink. I just can't control it. (Joan Yates)

> I overindulge in food, sex and alcohol. (Derek Crispin)

If you are too heavy for your height and build – if, for example, your waist measurement (measured directly over the navel) is bigger than your chest measurement (for either sex), or you know you have moved up one or two notches in clothes sizes in the last couple of years, or your thighs chafe together uncomfortably as you walk, or you sense areas of flesh vibrating when you walk or run which did *not* vibrate a year or two ago – you probably are taking in more food than you need. Regrettably, our metabolisms slow down as we age, and the food intake on which we were lean in our teens and twenties will make us heavier in our thirties, forties and fifties.

We need to make choices about it. Those choices do not have to be to be thin or to try to maintain the body-shape we had in our twenties through all the circumstances of our life, but they might be to notice if too much food is making us feel heavy, lethargic, or 'weighed down'.

If you are 'weighed down' by your body, look at why you are eating more than you need. Sometimes it is a matter of trying to fuel yourself through exhaustion or over-extension:

I'm inclined to eat now in case I get hungry later, [says Sian Adams]; I rush from pillar to post in my work and often miss regular mealtimes. I have found myself in a position of being famished and upset in the late afternoon or early evening. The mistake I tend to make now is to constantly fill up with food I don't need so as to avoid feeling hungry and panicky later. It's a metaphor for me for running out of steam, not being up to the task: so it all comes down to anxiety.

Derek and Joan eat more than they need for the sheer pleasure of eating – and indeed food is one of the great pleasures of life. There is no need for it to cease to be so, but you do need to take on board the fact that anything you eat and do not burn up you will find yourself wearing!

Not enough

Many women and some men chronically eat far too little because they are anxious to keep their weight low. Furthermore, many women and some men chronically eat far too little because they suffer from pressure and stress during the working day to an extent that it prevents them from eating.

As soon as I wake up during the week, I start to psych myself up for work [says a middle-aged senior accountant]. I have a cup of coffee and a cigarette. Once I hit the office there is no way I could face food. I keep going on coffee and cigarettes, have a couple of beers at lunch time, then have a big dinner when I get home at seven o'clock. It plays hell with my digestion and my weight fluctuates a lot.

Asked if this pattern ever varied he replied:

Yes, sometimes you might take a client out for lunch or they might take you out for lunch, in which case you are out for three hours or more eating an enormous, rich meal, and sitting long over the brandy. It's all very pleasant and civilized, but, I doubt it's the most healthy way to carry on. If it's somebody's birthday, or someone in the office leaves, we probably stay longer in the pub then, too, and drink more.

Looking at this in cold blood you might feel, what an obviously unhealthy way to carry on, but on reflection you may notice similarities with your own life. It is easy to get into a pattern like this when you feel under pressure, and if you are happy with it and your body is comfortable with it, fine. It *does* put stress on all your major functions to keep them fuelled by stimulants (coffee and cigarettes) and depressants (alcohol) all day. It *is* a macho display system, essentially, to make a statement: 'I am so important and busy I do not have time to eat. I am so stressed I could not possibly digest anything.'

'I can cope with sudden enormous overloads of food and alcohol' is a macho statement too. Again, if you find it exhilarating and it is a life-style that works well for you, fine; but if you do feel under pressure to live like this, and do not enjoy the stresses and the aftermaths, you may want to think about other choices.

> I eat grapefruit for breakfast, I'm full of coffee, starving and jittery by lunch, and lurch from 'bad' weeks where I give in and have pizza slices or bacon rolls for lunch, to 'good' weeks where I stick to salads and oranges. It's imperative to look good in my job, and my own self-confidence goes downhill if my clothes are tight because I've put on weight.

This is macho pressure working the other way round, where this highly qualified software designer of thirty-two is physically uncomfortable half her working day because of the necessity to keep her weight fashionably low. Naomi Wolf in *The Beauty Myth* (Vintage, 1991) has demonstrated that the glamorous imagery in which we are steeped, soaked and saturated encourages women to aspire to a body weight well below what would be normal and healthy. It is shocking to find that most women and, more horrifying still, many little girls, aspire to weigh the same sort of weights to which women and girls fell during the Dutch famine of 1943. In spite of her expertise Caroline (the software designer) feels that it is 'imperative to look good', because she has frequent contact with clients, but she also suspects that 'I often get taken out to lunch as a little light relief.'

She is caught in the double bind experienced by many women

who work hard to develop their skills and careers and then find they must work very hard at their appearance too, undertaking exercise regimes which are less about enjoying and strengthening the physique than about moulding its shape to fit the current macho fantasy of how a woman should be shaped, and having the constant hum of their daily calorie count distracting them from creative and positive work they might be doing.

Women in the workplace frequently feel under pressure to look thin, and also to look young. If you are not young you have to dress and behave as 'young' as possible. This is for the entirely macho reason that women are less threatening that way. If they are burning up energy maintaining their thinness and prettiness then they are less energetic as colleagues and potential rivals. If they look young, their knowledge and experience is less obvious, less challenging. What would a workplace full of robust, healthy, clever women who were spontaneous about food and unfussy about clothes be like? Very frightening for men, for a while. After a while, however, it would be marvellous for men too, because it would free them from the tedious business of their side of this: causing offence if you do admire a woman's appearance, causing offence if you do not, being required to be a genuine equal one minute and a gallant supporter the next, unable to form warm friendships or intellectual relationships with women colleagues in case they are misinterpreted, and all the rest of the sad muddle in which we currently find ourselves.

Digestion

We have already spoken of the stresses to the digestive system caused by radical on/off eating patterns. Let us think of other things. When did you last give any loving attention to your bowels? The chances are you never gave them a thought until you reached your early thirties or your first relatively senior post, whichever came first. For some of us, from then on, there are times when we seem rarely to think of anything else! It is because life gets so crowded and privacy so rare that this part of our natural rhythm can get unsettled:

There is a critical moment for me in the morning before I go out. If I miss that, I can't go to the loo till the next day! I could not possibly manage in the toilet at work – it is unisex and extremely un-private.

I do not know whether this inhibition is peculiar to the UK or not, but I do know that a surprising number of managers, when asked to reflect on their health, described constipation and piles resulting from literally not having time to go to the toilet. Often this was linked with lengthy commuting journeys – early departures and late returns home, and a sense of constant rush. If this is a problem for you, it is a sensible piece of body maintenance to sort it out – or to make space to let it sort itself out. In most cases all that is necessary is to make sure you have plenty of fibre in your diet, plenty of liquid intake (H_2O, not alcohol, which is dehydrating, or coffee which is diuretic), and to take your time in the loo. Take a book, read, relax, do not hurry. The gut is a very sensitive reactor to worry, stress, embarrassment, fear and joy. Adjusting your diet and not expecting your bowels to function according to a hectic and pre-set schedule is a decidedly good and gentle way of helping the body to be a strong, fit and resilient vehicle for the soul.

Allergies and addictions

Drinking too much alcohol is very macho – as we have already noticed. Men have been heard to be coerced by colleagues in the pub at lunch time by the contemptuous rejoinder, 'Oh, don't be a *girl*', when they order a non-alcoholic drink. In many organizational cultures drinking a great deal of alcohol together is an important part of the bonding process and there is a kind of 'respect' for a person who drinks heavily as though it demonstrates some sort of prowess or toughness.

This tends to work against women, because even if a woman is invited and included and does drink heavily, she compromises her all-important visual impact (both by looking less neat in the short term and damaging her skin and figure in the long term), and she compromises her working persona, since where a tipsy man is regarded as a rather dashing figure of mild amusement, a tipsy woman, unless the target of a specific seduction attempt, tends to be regarded with embarrassment and contempt.

Men and women who drink large quantities of alcohol risk addiction to a very dangerous drug. All the major body-systems are attacked in the end by over-use of alcohol. Behavioural disorders, emotional breakdown, and the severe disruption of relationships are also likely. Before getting this far down the line there is the dismal business of 'lost' afternoons when you cannot focus and concentrate because of lunchtime drinking, and the misery of waking dehydrated, nauseous and hung over. We all know this clearly and yet can still easily get pushed or led into drinking more than we meant to.

It is useful to think through some of the things that alcohol does for you, and to be able sometimes to find those functions in other ways. Is it a treat, a break, a small pleasure, a way of being nice to someone else? All those things can be done in other ways. The other line to take is to ask yourself whether you want to make your own decisions about how and when you use alcohol, or whether you are going to let other people dictate it to you. Once you get hold of it as your own choice, you will find it much easier to be assertive when you need to be.

Nicotine is the other legal drug to which many of us are addicted. As it also begins its entry into the body by mouth, we will address it here. Neil Glover's work, like so many people's, includes more and more writing as time goes on. He says, 'I chain-smoke when I write.'

When he writes at home it is worse:

> There are so many places in most offices now where you can't smoke that you do cut down through the day. Then at home, where you can smoke ad lib, you catch up.

Giving up smoking is a major undertaking but well worth while. As well as ceasing to damage your lungs and throat, once the worst of withdrawal symptoms are over, feeling far fitter, you regain exquisite sensitivity of smell and taste. Not only that, your pockets are literally weighed down with the money you are not donating to the tobacco industry.

Some women, as we have noted, develop allergies, including

irritating and time-consuming food allergies, apparently as an expression of vulnerability at a point in their careers when they have been required to batten down vulnerabilities of other kinds. Men go through this too:

> I am fed up with my pattern of stress-related food allergies: it means my yoga is not getting to all the areas of spirit that it should do. I would love to be free of allergy, but I can't just will it to go away. (Paul Norton)

Interestingly he links it with this:

> I would like to handle depression better. I would like to have a sense of worth centred more in myself and my family than in my achievements. I used to win affection by doing well on tests at school

– as though his dis-ease or un-ease is to do with where his emotional centre of gravity is.

Our higher allergy rates must have environmental connections too: we live in a more poisoned atmosphere and eat more poisoned food than any other generation so far. We need to be sensitive to all the facts to hear the message our allergies are giving us.

Good thinking

What is the good thinking one can find to enable our relationship with food (and drink and cigarettes) to be a harmonious one?

If you are feeling heavy and taking in too much food, sometimes it is useful to visualize food as packets of energy. An ear of corn, a segment of orange, is a packet of energy taken in from the sun, the rain, the nutrients in the soil and transformed. We then swallow it down and transform it into potential energy for ourselves. Looked at like this, it starts to feel less appealing to swallow down packets of energy you do not need, which will end up glued onto your body as packets of energy you will probably have slowed down too much to be able to use.

This concept has a profoundly vegetarianizing effect! Do you really want to swallow little bundles of energy that were frisking round a field or, worse, reared in the surreal horror of a battery farm? Maybe not. If what you really value about eating too much is the reward factor, or the companionship, or the sensual pleasure – you can have all those things in other ways.

If you eat too little, you can use the packets of energy idea too. Think of running the beautiful and precious organism of your body on too few packets of energy. You will clearly stress and harm it that way, and run down its organs and systems. Does it not feel more encouraging to think of giving it just enough to stay healthy and full of potential? Although it probably cannot be done suddenly, think of altering your personal style to allow your body to be its own appropriate size. Whether you are male or female, allow yourselves to absorb and consider the implications of a macho culture which requires women to aspire to the body-weight of a famine victim.

Talking of famine victims, I vividly remember being loomed over by a teacher at my primary school, me tearfully refusing to eat my pineapples and custard, and him exhorting me to 'think of all the little children who are starving'.

I had seen newspaper photographs of their poor distorted little bodies, but could not make any connection between that and my nausea at the time. Thirty-five years on, the children of the Third World still starve to death, and we can watch it happening live by satellite on TV any night of the week. Why this does not solve all our food problems at a stroke I do not know, but it does not. It is, however, worth noticing as we grapple with all our feelings about food and nourishment, that having enough food to stay alive without any struggle is a First-World privilege of which we should be aware.

Sleep

Being tired is an adult epidemic. As a child you hear it continually as the reasons why adults will not do all kinds of things; as an adult with responsibilities it suddenly becomes part of the everyday texture of life.

Sleep patterns can quickly be distorted by worry, and the edge of worry may be sharpened by being in unfamiliar surroundings.

Julia Primera an industrial psychologist aged thirty-eight, says:

> After my son was born and I returned to work, I started to suffer from insomnia, especially when I was away in hotel rooms. The bleakness of being awake at 3 and 4 o'clock in the morning and wondering how the hell I was going to cope the next day was terrible.

Joan Yates lost a lot of sleep in the final bout of opposition which preceded her very satisfying career move. When her worries caught up with her, she says:

> I tried to use my yoga to un-tense myself. Sometimes it worked and sometimes it didn't. I went through the breathing and relaxation routine to try to stop my mind racing and to unclench my body.

Travelling a great deal can disrupt your sleep patterns too, whether you are going through actual time zones or not. Travelling home by car after running intense courses or pursuing concentrated and combative discussion, I have found very dangerous because of being tremendously preoccupied with the details and nuances of the day: so far I have been lucky, and terrifying both myself and whoever I nearly drove into has been sufficient to reawaken me to the reality of driving and the need to take care.

The other hazard I have found is being overtaken by profound sleepiness quite suddenly while ploughing up a motorway. Seductive little dreams flicker at the corner of your eyes and seep upwards from the lower range of vision to pull your eyelids downwards. The car veers, if you are lucky, onto the rough lane marker whose noise wakes you up, if you are unlucky, into someone else. It is imperative to try to plan your journeys so that you have a calming- down or debriefing process at the end of an intense session, and are less likely to drive into someone through being mentally removed from the situation; and it is also important to plan for a short stop for sleep and/or strong coffee at service stations to avoid the appalling risk of dozing off at the wheel.

Intense overwork can lead you to being exhausted, but too revved up to sleep; or it may just wipe you out. Mark Ellis says:

> In my last job I worked a fifteen-hour day and was no use to anyone. I have four children aged between seven and thirteen and I never saw them. I had no energy left for anything at all.

Simon Ayres's sleep pattern has asserted itself in an inconvenient way:

> I wake tremendously early and when I get home after a day's work I just want to sleep or flop. I'm mostly very tired.

When you are in Mark Ellis's situation, the first thing you have to do is acknowledge that it is happening, and then, in whatever way is possible, seize a piece of time in which to think it over. Is that the balance you want in your life? If not, it is important to make plans and adjustments, be they minor or major, to shift that balance to something you are at least a little more comfortable with. If your sleep pattern, like Simon's, has settled in an unwelcome way, you can look to adjusting it by changing your patterns of exercise, fresh air, alcohol intake and so forth. You can also, like Joan, use systematic relaxation techniques to cope with inconvenient periods of wakefulness – they may lull you back to sleep or they may simply release you into a peaceful way of experiencing that wakefulness. If none of those things make any difference, a positive option is to try to find ways of enjoying your wakeful time: to appreciate watching the sun coming up, to get a great stock of novels or thrillers and lie around reading indulgent stuff you would not normally allow yourself during those wakeful hours, to write your journal or dream your daydreams or have a long gentle bath. Beware, though, of having insomniac treats that involve alcohol:

> For nights and nights I woke at 3 or 4 in the morning, and lay, worrying about work, tossing and turning. I started to get up and have a stiff whisky to get myself back to sleep. After another week or two I suddenly noticed I was waking up *in order to have the whisky*! (Sian Adams)

Do not set up patterns of need like this as you will only disrupt your life further.

Because of the strain of multiple commitments, some parents (usually the mother) who work outside the home as well as in it, are outrageously tired. Society has no respect whatever for the task of child-rearing and if you are doing other work you are supposed to make your child-care efforts simply disappear from sight. Many women and some men find themselves stranded in the appalling double shift of family and career or shipwrecked in the deprivation of having their job taken away from them completely while they look after young children. What we all need is more flexible ways to work; but in terms of culture and legislation we are going to have a long wait. This means that every parent and every family has to be extremely ingenious in finding ways of balancing their energies. It is important not to be harassed by bogus rhetoric about being serious about your career or about being a bad/good parent, but to try to tune in to what you, your partner and your children need financially, can manage spiritually and emotionally, and feel is best for you. Because children, and partnerships and the economic climate change, working opportunities change too, so you probably need to review your choices frequently. Being appallingly tired does *not* have to be a price for having children and interesting work. That is the point to bear in mind.

One last consideration about tiredness: if you are chronically fatigued and exhausted and cannot explain it, i.e. there does not seem to be an excessive amount of effort in your current life, you have had a medical check to rule out such things as viral infection or anaemia, then your tiredness may be a metaphor for something else. Concealing our own feelings from ourselves is exhausting. If you are tired and do not understand why, allow yourself some chance to think broadly about your life. Is there something you need to attend to or change? Is there something you are longing to do and not allowing yourself to notice? Reflect and listen to your inner voice: it may have something fascinating to suggest to you.

Pushing relentlessly on through exhaustion may be macho, but it is far from intelligent. Tiredness needs your understanding, your action, and your creative response to be resolved positively.

Exercise

It is well-documented now that regular exercise improves our lives in every way. Reducing the risk of strokes and coronaries, keeping body-weight favourable, and preserving muscle tone and bone mass, can be added to the beneficial levelling of mood-swings, helping to put work problems into a less frantic perspective and balancing out sleep and insomnia. In a macho culture the twin problems are that it is easy to become so pressured and so busy that you do not feel you have any time for exercise at all, or that you select a form of exercise that is in itself highly stressful, competitive, and demanding. Being in a sporting and competitive situation that you experience as *fun* is fine; a similar situation that starts to feel like yet another worry, yet another pressure, is not useful. Siobhan Boyle says,

> I would like to go running more. I work from 9 till 6, and all the rest of the time I'm out doing things I enjoy, and running gets pushed out.

If your schedule presently feels so crowded that you never have time for exercise, consider whether you would like to alter this and make some space. Even one session a week of stretching, or stamina work, or intelligently worked out cross training will make a real difference to your strength and well-being – or a ten-minute spot per day can lift your fitness.

David Britton says:

> I gave up all organized sport five years ago because of time pressures, but I spend five minutes every morning doing sit-ups and press-ups, and I run around and play with the kids.

Derek Crispin says he does the military close-confinement exercises every day (any irony in the title of this choice seems to pass him completely by). If closely confined is what your life is, then this is a particularly appropriate training set. The regime consists of:

- On waking:
- 10 rotations of the arms forwards
- 10 rotations of the arms backwards

- 10 stretch and waist pivots right and left
- 10 squats
- 10 touch alternate toes
- 30 press-ups (forehead to touch the ground)
- 10 rolling press-ups
- 25 squat thrusts
- 10 bicycles

Derek says,

> I gave up rugby two years ago because I didn't have time any more. Up until then I was very aerobically fit. Now I do the close-confinement work every day. I used to think about the Iran hostages and hope they knew this set of exercises because it would have been such a help to them.

(Apparently the hostages did work as hard as they could on staying fit.)

Paul Norton and Joan Yates prefer yoga and cross-training to the fitness programmes centred largely on muscular strength and cardiovascular work. The oriental disciplines of yoga, tai chi, or the 'hard' martial arts (karate, tae kwon do, kung fu) may provide a valuable yin/yang balance when woven into a very head-centred Western way of living. The form of fitness they provide is not quite the same as Western gym/sport fitness. In addition to flexibility and cardiovascular improvement, they develop a deep awareness of breathing, and also the concept of paradoxical gentle strength described at the beginning of the book. The inclusiveness of their philosophy can spread to all aspects of your life.

Whichever type of exercise you choose, formal or informal, will bring you physical and mental refreshment and will probably also bring you into contact with a different selection of people from your family and your job. Consider finding some time, however little, to give to positive exercise, ensuring that it truly is not a task which will make your life more stressful, but that it will genuinely enhance it.

Anxiety

Derek Crispin said:

> If you had asked me to define stress a year ago, I would have said it was something that happens to people who are weak. Now I find that it is something that can happen to anyone, including me.

We know that stress is a modern epidemic. We know that neither our work practices nor our life practices are humane in that frequently they do not take into account the entire range of human capabilities and human needs and regularly require us to obliterate or amputate bits of our physical, intellectual or emotional selves. Failure to do so is often, as Derek says, regarded as weak. As his family has increased and his business life has grown more complex, he has found stress can be part of his life too.

> I got a shock discovering that my blood pressure had got very high. For a time I was working long hours ineffectively, but I have made a real effort to get organized and work effectively for shorter hours and then make a good separation between myself and worries associated with work.

Keeping work worries in their appropriate place is important to Parminder Sharma too:

> Stress comes and goes, but I switch off well. I'm not sure I could do it if I had a family to look after as well, but I can look after myself. I'm pushing *all* my resources into my career, so I have to let off steam, and I make sure I do.

Being able to 'switch off', to arrange not to be swamped by work-worry when there is nothing you can usefully do about it is of prime importance in avoiding stress burn-out. What are your strategies? Do you have a trusted friend with whom you can confide, a journal into which you can off-load when no one is available to listen, an absorbing sport or hobby which enables you to forget everything else for the interludes while you take part in it, a sense of yourself as a person separate from your working identity when that is what you need? Have time to think these through and note and assimilate anything that you would prefer to be different.

Simple good planning can be a factor in cutting down stress. Joan Yates remarks that 'It made a striking difference to my stress levels to limit the number of meetings I arrange per week.'

Meetings beget meetings beget report-writing beget the need for action. They also work the bits of you that respond to other people, cope with aggression, explain ideas, defend territory, take initiatives. There is only so much of that you can do per day, or per week. The macho pressure is to say I can do any amount of anything that anyone cares to throw at me. An interesting alternative is to say, if I take control of my workload I can do what I select extremely effectively and delegate the rest. Think through your own pattern. Are you afraid to regulate your workload, afraid ever to say 'no' in case it makes you look weak? You may be and come over as much tougher in the long run if you make judicious choices about activities and priorities, and conserve your energy by limiting the stress of overload.

Any pleasure you get from your work will increase your tolerance of pressure. Angela Winters says:

> Ironically, this job is harder and more stressful than my last, but my health is very good because I am enjoying what I do.

Neil Glover points out:

> When I was a teacher I rarely got through a term without an illness of some sort, but since starting my new job I have not been ill at all.

It is worth noticing that the happier you are, the more resilient you are too. Unfortunately, it is not possible for everyone to find work which fulfils rather than stifles them in an institution or organization which enables rather than crushes them. If you do not derive much happiness at work it is a crucial and much undervalued skill in stress management to make small episodes of happiness throughout the day.

Michael Groves knows that he is particularly susceptible to

stress and is always alert, and he speaks here with characteristic honesty:

> There is schizophrenia and manic depression in my family, as well as neurological problems. Because of this I watch out for signs of hyper in myself. I notice that my weight drops sharply when my anxiety increases – and the anxiety itself I regard as a symptom of the sick organization.
>
> I cope with the danger of this anxiety by being aware, and by making occasions for pleasure, if possible every day. For instance, today I am meeting a friend for a drink after work. I will spend an hour or so with him relaxing. I 'ought' to work late, and if I don't do that I 'ought' to go home to my wife, but I'm going to do what *I* need and just unwind for a short time.

Knowing your own risks is important – knowing yourself well enough to understand what may tip you over the edge enables you to counter particularly anxious situations with rest and relaxation. Constructive selfishness like Michael's, an ability to put your own needs if not always first at least somewhere on the map can provide you with the stress-antidotes you need.

Anxiety can shoot up the graph when your body asks you for more attention than it is easy to give when you are doing a pressurizing job. It could be through actual illness, or it could be ordinary and healthy but demanding parts of your life-cycle, like pregnancy, or the menopause or simply the results of your fifty-year health check giving you pause for thought.

> I had a major operation for the removal of a stomach ulcer. It was the first time I'd ever been in hospital, and the first time I'd ever had a big operation. I'm slimmer now and eat better. It was a stress-related ulcer – not entirely because of the pressure of my present job, but because of the way I had absorbed tensions and pressures for long periods of time before that. I work long hours now and I work very hard but I *don't internalize the pressure so much.* (Chris Hargreaves)

Chris's language is interesting, in that his anxiety at one point literally got right inside him and made him very ill, but he is managing a very difficult job now by *not* internalizing the anxiety it engenders.

Cara Frances's pregnancy with her first child coincided with a major upheaval in her industry:

> I was pregnant and the company was sold out from under me. I was very tired, very pressurized, and fearful of being unwell and absent because of the pile-up of work and because of not being there to defend my patch. Two babies due in that company at that time were born five weeks premature – mine was one of them. I think there must be a link between that and the pressure we were under. The other woman told me she remembered thinking strongly 'I wish I didn't have to go to work on Monday' and her baby was born on the Sunday night. The other day a colleague who is pregnant now told me how just the thoughts of getting on the train in the rush hour made her want to cry, and it took me right back to how I felt when I was expecting Elizabeth.

The macho pregnancy is an eighties phenomenon which put atrocious pressure on both women and men. In order to maintain their professional identity at all, women rising into management found that if they planned to have a family too they had little in the way of supportive legislation and much in the way of their pregnancy being used as a good excuse to sideline them. The only option seemed to be to tough the pregnancy out, deny it as much as possible, set a ludicrously early return date and, essentially, tear oneself apart. The havoc this wreaked among the women trying to produce this front, and their male partners trying to support them when in the privacy of home they panicked and despaired about keeping it all up, has done nothing at all for equal opportunities and a great deal to hazard women and men's and babies' physical emotional health. It is essential to create a climate where more flexible and creative work patterns can be developed for both women and men while they also do the work of parenting. If you or your partner are pregnant or considering a pregnancy, do have some time to do good planning with plenty of alternative strategies written in to cover some of the different ways you may find you feel. Try not to get cornered into minimizing the pregnancy and the baby, nor into being entirely taken over by them. If you can share thoughts and experiences with other parents in similar situations it may help – once the barriers are down, you will probably find they are making complicated arrangements and adjustments too.

Finding constructive working solutions to anxiety-provoking issues like these is always important work, and should be generously networked and shared.

A shift in personal philosophy can ease anxiety. Somewhat unexpectedly, given his down-to-earth attitude, Mark Ellis expressed an intention to 'learn to meditate'. In fact meditation is a very down-to-earth and sensible skill to learn, since it provides interludes of profound detachment, and a good foundation of inner calm. Finally, Phoebe Driscoll points out what she believes can truly keep anxiety at bay:

> We should not measure ourselves by other people's standards – women in particular do this a lot and rate themselves according to other people's evaluation of them. We should measure ourselves by how our achievements match up with our own ambitions and goals.

Well-being

TRIGGER EIGHT:
Think about your own well-being and have some moments to affirm and celebrate anything you find to be positively pleased by.

I was quite ill as a child, but my health improved a lot when I reached the age of eleven. Now I'm forty-five. I don't smoke, and I drink in moderation. I'm eleven and a half stone, and really I'm pleased to weigh the same and be the same shape as I was when I was twenty. (David Britton)

My health is good – I am a fit agile person. (Parminder Sharma)

My health is tip-top. I am most pleased with my resilience in health terms. (Phoebe Driscoll)

I am pleased not to have gone under with all the stress this job imposes. The rumours surrounding me last year were pure poison... I am glad to be resilient. (Siobhan Boyle)

Being pleased about small, specific strands of well-being can accumulate eventually into a positive health awareness in which we are very definitely fit enough to survive.

5. 'Do as I do'

Perhaps it has not crossed your mind that you are a role model, but undoubtedly once you are in management, you have become one. Juniors will consciously or unconsciously imitate aspects of the way you behave and, if they find you impressive, so will peers and seniors. In fact, being a good role model is one of the most powerful ways in which you can influence the organization in which you work:

TRIGGER EIGHT:

In what ways are you a good role model? What quality or behaviour of yours would you like people to imitate?

The macho model of leadership and management has been passed down by role-modelling and imitation, essentially from military culture. Toughness begets toughness and that is fine, but insensitivity begets insensitivity and that is less desirable. Great military leaders seem to have managed to combine a tough and demanding attitude with a carefully judged and sparingly used capacity for tenderness. Their lesser imitators are inclined to reproduce the harshness but be incapable of seeing the times and places where gentleness is more appropriate.

Performing to the best of your own ability, and getting the best out of other people, requires a whole spectrum of behaviours, used responsively and intelligently according to circumstances. The people around you will undoubtedly find it useful to experience you behaving in a variety of different ways and to assess and adopt what suits them.

You may not be able to model everything you would wish. We would all like to be serene, resourceful, and brilliantly creative, but it may not be possible artificially to take on those qualities. It is useful, however, to collect up your good qualities in your mind, and to bear in mind that by embodying these you are giving other people an opportunity to be that way too. When

Siobhan Boyle thinks about this question, at first she feels she has nothing to offer:

> I'm not a good role model. I'm too individual. Also people are intimidated by my ability – I expect terrific pace and rate of work and put massive hours in. I criticize too much, I never give people enough strokes. I don't suffer fools gladly.

Well – that is a tough and macho profile, but when she thinks further, she has a balance to offer.

> I do think it is good that people can see me as a single woman having a really good time. I'm moving from parenthood to singleness. I think it's good for people to see me doing that really positively and well.

Consider whether your performance tends towards the intimidatory or the threatening, and if it does, simply let that thought stay in your mind for a while and see whether you want to change it.

As in the adage, 'Don't do as I say, do as I do', role-modelling cuts from theory to practice in corporate or organizational affairs. Everyone knows what the rule book or the mission statement says, but equally everybody knows 'how we do things around here', and there may well be a reality gap between the two. Staff hate being told 'we are all one big happy family', if we aren't, 'my door is always open', if it is not, and 'we always aim for excellence', if that is patently untrue. Such inconsistencies will de-motivate them more quickly than almost anything else. Behaviour which is coherent with what you say you are doing is worth its weight in gold and will be imitated down the line. Behaviour which actively improves on the standard 'this is how we do things around here', will be valued and emulated too. Thus you have an opportunity to change the culture without changing official policy or changing the rule book, by influencing the practice. Role-modelling can be seen as to do with demonstrating and passing down professional skills, or to do with demonstrating and passing down personal qualities. Some activities will overlap the two.

Role-modelling professional skills

David Britton believes that there are three distinct but interwoven qualities that he particularly models. The first is simple but crucial:

> I'm a good finisher. I don't have projects hanging around. I'm very tidy and organized and am able to work long hours, so I have an ability to push things through and get them done.

Anyone around him will be affected by the tidiness, the organization, and the sense that things get done on time. He is unlikely to have to try to enforce tidiness or promptness since his colleagues will be in the habit of assuming that this is how things are. If good self-management is taken for granted in him, he is in a position to expect it to be so among his colleagues, and a beneficent (rather than a vicious) circle will evolve which will be favourable for the whole organization because there will be a genuine sense that people mean what they say about commitments and deadlines and will take responsibility for themselves. We have probably all worked in places where the *opposite* is true, so it is interesting to reflect on how we would feel about being in the sort of working atmosphere which David generates.

His second point is a very interesting one:

> I don't believe in stars, I believe in teams. I believe I am good at developing teams. There are twenty-eight people in my European network and I have ensured and made it possible for them all to know and respect one another.

Would you like to work in a true team where you genuinely make common cause together, or do you prefer the potentially creative cut and thrust of splits and factions? Or, indeed, are you accustomed to being a star? If you grew up as Paul Norton did, and as many 'high achievers' do, 'winning affection by doing well in tests at school', you may have a fairly strong compulsion to be a 'star'. It may be quite a surprise to notice that there could be ways of operating effectively in a group other than dominating it or bidding for domination of it. In the last analysis I do not think it is sensible to say that every person should wish to be an integrated team member and nobody should want to be a star. Clearly nobody who wants to be a star should work for David Britton unless they are going to topple him and introduce a different culture into that group. Nevertheless, it is interesting to notice what the implications of starhood are, and compare them with the implications of teamness. Starhood has always been a macho, a yang quality, because it has to do not with shining, but out-shining others. It suggests having more space, more clout, more leeway for idiosyncrasies and unfairness, more license, more privilege and more attention. It also means having more danger, more exposure, more risk, more stress. High-profile stardom is a masculine thing: that is one reason why most of the people at the top of most organizations, including organizations which have an overwhelmingly female membership, are men.

Team-working is yin behaviour – sharing, meshing, identifying collectively and not singly, helping, being flexible, co-operating, pooling. The benefits are solace, protection, support and, on paper anyway, a greater potential energy to go into the task in hand, as less is expended in holding position, managing internal splits and surviving pressure. Single ownership of ideas, successes and failures, is transformed into collective ownership. There may be little individual glory when things go well, but there will be little personal recrimination when things go wrong. This blending of boundaries and overall fluidity is a *yin* way to do business. Reflect on whether you have ever had an opportunity to work this way, and if so, what you felt about it, whether you enjoyed the belonging and support, or whether you suffered from a sense of anonymity.

Perhaps the most creative position would be to be aware of the two polarities – a star-based culture, and a team-based culture – and to be able to move between these two polarities as you need to during your career.

The particularly valuable thing about David Britton is how clear and transparent he is about what he is doing. He runs an integrated team because he believes that is the best way to get the job done, and is quite open about his plan and intention. The team values and the openness underpin the third piece of professional behaviour on his part which he believes is a positive role model.

> I would like other people to emulate my honesty. I have a low level of political activity [he means corporate politics]. I don't do anything naughty politically.

His sense of self-disciplined integrity within an organization which is, actually, rife with internal politics, is an impressive example of gentle strength. Being true to his own principles protects him from involvement in all sorts of coups and counter-coups which would compromise him and his team, and also earns him a degree of respect which means he operates with relative immunity to internal politicking himself.

Joan Yates also believes that her efficiency sets a valuable example within her department. The rationale for it is a *yin*, collective one:

> I try desperately hard not to let people down, so planning is very important to me. I am thorough, organized and efficient.

She is not efficient principally to enhance her own image, but to make sure that she is a good team member and does not complicate or hold up anybody else's work.

The theme of honest communication is an important piece of role-modelled behaviour for many people. It is often in reaction against *not* being treated with honesty by superiors in the past. Remember the appointment made on the basis of the candidate speaking a non-existent language? (p.20) It has confirmed Leonard Rawlins's commitment:

> It's important to me to role-model integrity: and that means things like *not* swinging it by lies about non-existent languages, and it means practising what you preach.

Parminder Sharma extends being honest into being honest about aspects of herself:

> I am very direct and honest, I have lots of energy and lots of skills but I have weaknesses which I can be frank about too.

There is a paradoxical strength in clearly owning weaknesses. It does *not* work this way if it is done as a coy pose, or with any hint of fishing for a complimentary contradiction, but if it is a genuine acknowledgement of yin and yang, strength and weakness, then it is an empowering piece of role-modelling. It clearly states that everyone makes mistakes, that it is dignified and sensible to acknowledge them, that weaknesses can be shared and discussed and learning and developmental opportunities can be derived from such discussions. If a junior sees a respected senior able to behave in this way, they are enabled to behave this way too, rather than to cover up and evade dealing with any difficulties they do have.

Derek Crispin emphasizes being a good, articulate communicator as a key quality he wants to pass on by example:

> I think I am a popular leader because I communicate well. It is clear to juniors that that is basic to my popularity and if they want to be popular too, which most people do, they will probably take it up as a good way to do things.

Cara Frances extends communication to an ability to delegate. Her experience shows that a linked sequence from self-management to communication to delegation makes her efficient in a way that she feels sets a valuable example:

> I think prioritizing is the first step, organizing yourself in a general way so that you are not bogged down, and then communicating, delegating, and *involving* your subs. Explain to them *where* things fit the vision.

Her point about helping everyone to understand where their contribution fits in is important. Divide and rule is a macho principle where you are keeping information and power parcelled up for yourself and a few chosen others. It is much more *yin* and feminine and co-operative to share information as a way of getting people to work, rather than to withhold information as a way of getting people to work. The safeness or unsafeness of doing so in your organization needs to be weighed, but without a doubt someone like Cara in a senior position being open with information and interpreting openly the overall plan, will influence her juniors to do that when they reach a senior level themselves – or at the very least to know that that is a viable leadership option.

Mark Ellis shares David Britton's view about the importance of teams. The strength which he feels may be a good role for others is: 'I can mould a consensus'.

What a gift: any of us who have worked in a team where there was no consensus, where people were off on their own private crusades every five minutes, fervently wish we had a manager like Mark. Even more interestingly, Mark feels he moulds a consensus not by cracking the whip, but by:

> Mutual respect. There is nothing so important as relationships with others. There must be respect for their genuine feelings and for your own too. You must pay attention to the people and you must pay attention to the task, and that is how you get things going in the right direction.

Working for someone who gets group loyalty through mutual respect is likely to produce future managers who also do things that way.

A fascinating example of mutual respect appearing on the agenda during the training period is the medical model. Having given birth to five children spread out between 1970 and 1990 I have been the lucky recipient of every medical fashion in between and followed with growing delight the changes. In 1970 both doctors and midwives were the owners of all the information and expertise, performed coercive and invasive (and unnecessary) procedures (enemas, pubic shaves, rectal examinations) without any preamble at all, let alone asking permission or giving explanation, and after delivering the baby gave it to you some time later as a huge favour, as if it was a present you did not deserve but out of their great good-heartedness they might allow you to keep. In 1990, doctors and midwives all introduced themselves in first-name terms, consulted your wishes at every point, explained every single thing they did, and clearly saw themselves in alliance with yourself. However, you did not doubt that *you* were the one giving birth, not them, and the baby arrived in your arms within seconds of slithering out. In my experience, certainly in normal deliveries where the risks are low, a huge movement has taken place in the last twenty years to take the macho out of maternity care. Delivery is no longer done to you by medical staff, it is something where you join your energies with theirs and do together. This synergy or synthesis is a wonderful example of a non-macho way of getting through a demanding and stressful challenge.

Professional skills themselves can be passed on by example. Chris Hargreaves's belief that 'problems are there to be solved', gives his whole operation a positive feel, and his staff a positive mind-set.

Paul Norton wants his own meticulous professional enquiry to be the quality his students and colleagues 'pick up' from being around him:

> I want to show that things *can* be thought about and understood, *can* be made sense of and responded to: it's a sustaining and human world out there. If I can show people how to think about accounts of experience, they will have a better understanding of morality, politics, and experience itself: it is not all some mysterious muddle. We have a responsibility towards enquiry and a responsibility towards each other.

Paul is expressing an integrity of intention and an excellence of practice within his own field. Of course this is applicable in any field at all. If your boss's own work is excellent and meticulous, it is likely to inspire you, create a climate in which you will set yourself very high standards too. When you are in the leadership role yourself, without a doubt your own commitment to excellence will filter down through your staff.

Role-modelling personal qualities

The crossover between models of good professional practice and positive personal qualities is in the sense of being able to join energy and effort with colleagues:

> I'm not conscious of being a role model, but I do try to be enabling of my staff rather than intimidating towards them. (Sean McCann)

Displaying personal qualities which *enable* those around you rather than intimidate them is crucial. Personal qualities which make other people feel inadequate are part of the profile of the macho manager. Siobhan Boyle felt that her professional pyrotechnics tended to inhibit her colleagues, but that her personal experiences and her way of carrying these off could well be useful path-finding for them. Some other managers' sense of where they set an example bridges the area between professional skills and personal qualities. Simon Ayres cites:

> I have an ability to get things done while still being interesting. I hope this shows that you *can* be imaginative and creative and still get things done.

His example is a broad one, a kind of lateral thinking which challenges the narrow view of efficiency as performing only in one way. Juniors working with him have an opportunity to observe that, to use the vernacular, there are more ways than one to skin a cat. It is immensely useful when faced with a problem to have seen that a good outcome can be obtained by taking creative and original courses for their solution as well as obvious ones.

Janet King's position is similar in that she wants to make clear that you can reconcile two priorities that might be seen as contradictory.

> It's important to me to have absolute integrity and to have high expectations on performance too. The one does not exclude the other. You can do both.

She sets an example where cutting corners is not acceptable where both the means and the ends must be correct. If she herself meets her obligations, keeps up with deadlines and solves problems as necessary, without lowering her own standards, anyone in her orbit has a chance to witness it. They will certainly be affected in some way, and consciously or unconsciously may seek to imitate. The commitment to overall quality is a non-macho thing: it is similar to the sharing and teamworking scenario, in that it involves being prepared to pour energy into the common good, the common weal, rather than channelling it all into self-promotion.

In many careers, the underlying aim of the work is the common cause into which energies should go:

> I'd like people to pick up from me a commitment to the values that underpin what we're doing. (Chris Hargreaves)

– rather than into purely individual career development.

Managers often take all the air time. They feel they should issue instructions, give explanations, make plans, solve problems, dispense information and take initiatives. All this pro-activity is very macho. The better manager may well be the one who knows how to listen. As Neil Glover says:

> I see it as important to role-model being a good listener. I try to listen thoughtfully, and I try not to be defensive.

This means listening properly, empathetically, with involvement. It also means having the yin strength to hear suggestions or criticisms without tensing up and becoming defensive.

Cara Frances points out that your staff tell you more if they feel they can:

> I try to be approachable, not stand-offish, genuinely open to news, views and input from staff.

She is a boss who does not hide behind an authoritative persona in order to avoid learning material, pleasing or not so pleasing, from sources within her organization. As such, she shows others how it can be done: how openness and apparent undefendedness can be a strength, not a weakness. Good listening, where receptiveness is combined with equilibrium and poise, allows both the individual and the organization to grow. A richer persona than the archetypal authority-figure can be found when a manager is not afraid to be funny.

> Although I am totally dedicated, I try to be so in a way that's not horribly earnest. I laugh a lot, and do not show how uptight I might be. Everyone perceives me as 'calm' even though I am often churning inside. (Joan Yates)

Humour eases the atmosphere around her hectic and committed projects and deflates any suspicion that she might be self-important. It is a valuable safety valve and, in her case, a rather reassuring quality which allows her staff some distance from her anxiety when it does arise.

Michael Groves quite specifically cites humour as a way of levelling out staff hierarchies and demonstrating alternatives to macho attitudes:

> I use humour a lot: I laugh at myself as well as at others. It's part of treating everyone equally, and not pre-judging people. I learn from other people's mistakes, and I expect others to learn from my errors. I know that I'm actually quite an important man to some of the men I know, particularly young men, because I can project the feminine side, I can create a 'softer' image and still be masculine.

Heterosexual men in a homophobic culture have problems showing their sensitivity, softness and creativity, because this is so quickly labelled as homosexual. Homosexual and bisexual men face a barrage of paranoia and prejudice and their sensitivity and flair may also be stereotyped and not appreciated for its intrinsic value. It is anxiety about our own sexual identity and boundaries which makes us keen to label others: we all need to be alive to this tendency both as an obligation to our fellow humans, and as part of unscrambling our attitudes to Equal Opportunities. Man who can role-model a typical 'female' behaviour and women who can role-model a typical 'male' behaviour (by which I mean things like brilliance in mathematics and ease with technology, rather than ersatz macho aggression), are useful to us and our teams in allowing *all* the abilities of the team to come to the fore, not just the selection which fit people's sexually stereotyped preconceptions.

Your most important piece of role-modelling might be a personal priority of your own.

> I have an ability to take risks, not careless risks, but calculated risks. I'm hungry for knowledge – a seeker, someone who has the ability to change. I'm fascinated by people who can shift and grow and change things. I'd like to be a full and rounded person but not overwhelming. (Parminder Sharma)

Thus anyone around Parminder has an opportunity to see her always pushing for new ideas, new discoveries, not afraid to try new things. She also is aware of the need for a certain grace or tact which would stop her from becoming an inhibiting factor to other people by overwhelming them.

Leonard Rawlins knows that, paradoxically, you can influence a situation more by controlling it less:

> I try to role-model a belief system where one of the beliefs is that people should make up their own minds about things.

Because of his attitude, anyone who works for him will know that it is possible to be in charge, but still to allow others autonomy.

When you have considered what your own strong behaviours are which may be picked up and imitated by others, you may be pleased. Is there anything you want to change and adjust? It is possible to make gradual changes without feeling self-conscious. It may be valuable to you, your colleagues, and your organization, to make changes if you are projecting a way of behaving both professionally and as a person which you would *not* feel comfortable for others to follow.

Being a good role model in the end means making high standards and expertise seem achievable to anyone prepared to work for them, with an attitude that is respectful and generous:

> Radiance encourages people, but outshining everyone else inhibits them.
>
> (John Heider, *The Tao of Leadership*, p. 115)

The manager who sets the tone and example which brings out the best in his or her staff, then, is *radiant*.

6. **Moving mountains: Motivation and conflict resolution**

You can have a workforce with excellent skills and experience, but they are no use to you at all if you cannot motivate them; and they are little use if you are unable to take a lead in the positive resolution of clashes and conflicts which arise. The macho model of motivation is basically that you scare people into doing what you want them to do with the encouraging thought in addition that if they work hard enough, one day they will be in a position to push other people around just as you are pushing them around now. The macho model of conflict resolution is that the stronger or more devious party wins. Some version of natural selection takes place and the stronger or more cunning people end up at the top of the pile; and this is considered to be beneficial to the company, aiding its survival among other companies in the macho marketplace.

It is useful to take some time to consider what *really* motivates people, and therefore how we can best motivate ourselves and others. It is useful to look at the converse, too, at what demotivates people: how we can avoid becoming de-motivated ourselves, and how we can avoid our staff losing their motivation.

TRIGGER TEN:

What motivates you most of at the moment? Which factors demotivate you? How do you feel you best motivate other people? Do you ever de-motivate other people? In what way?

Make a note (mental or literal) of your answers to these questions and notice particularly anything unexpected in your response. On reflection, few people respond well to being frightened into compliance, or to having conflicts sorted out by a trial of strength. They appreciate instead a combination of quality of work with clear setting of boundaries.

Self-motivation

There is also a degree to which both as motivators and as motivatees, imaginative managers see the responsibility as lying within the individual themselves, and not within their boss. Phoebe Driscoll, for instance, asserts, 'I do feel that people should do some of their own motivational house-keeping.'

Interestingly, so long as the organizational culture supports this, i.e. so long as everybody sees peers doing likewise, people can very effectively take care of motivating themselves. A beneficent circle can arise where autonomy, busyness, and pro-activity are expected and supported. Is this how things are in your place of work? Or is there a tendency to see people who work hard, take initiatives and see things through quickly, as creeps and swots? Ask yourself what the prevailing attitude around you is at this moment.

It is a great revelation when you get hold of your own desire to motivate yourself. Parminder Sharma recounts how it happened for her:

> I used to keep a little notice by my bed which said, 'Expect a miracle today'. It was a year before I realized I had to create the [expletive deleted] miracle myself!

That moment changed Parminder's life, and in particular her attitude to her career, which, since she took to 'creating the miracle' herself, has gone from strength to strength.

Motivating factors

Apart from your own inspiration, what factors in your working life motivate you? It is interesting how few people mention money when asked this question directly. People do not like to be underpaid, but they have a far more intense dislike of being *undervalued*. What actually gets people up in the morning and moving with energy is a sense of purpose:

> I like contributing to something worth doing. It feels good believing that I am going to be able to deal with challenges as they arise. Money is important to me, but so is intellectual challenge and being part of a team moving towards a common goal. (Sean McCann)

Chris Hargreaves states his sense of being turned on by a task worth doing:

> I like facing a challenge where it's worth being able to achieve the goals set.

Some people really like the challenge to be considerable:

> I need to be stretched. I can't bear being less than on the edge of possibility. I don't perform well when I'm comfortable: but then I can create that adrenaline artificially if I need to.

Phoebe Driscoll is here practising what she preaches and doing her own motivational housekeeping, by good self-diagnosis and taking care of her own needs.

Siobhan Boyle prefers to be on the leading edge too:

> I like commitment, I find it re-energizing and fun. I like the challenge of doing something that no one's done before.

One of Siobhan's recurrent worries – shared by many other energetic and creative people – is that every organization she works for seems to want to swallow her up and digest her energy into itself, leaving her less radical, less innovative, and with less impetus and momentum. Hence her desire to continue to innovate. Her most recent assignment, to set up a women's project on the Gaza strip, would seem to fulfil abundantly the need for 'a challenge that no one's ever done before'.

Variety is the key turn-on factor for some managers:

> Variety motivates me. I like to be involved in the individual's process of change. (Simon Ayres)

> I like new things, new people, and new environments. (Neil Glover)

If variety is important to you, it is worth noticing that that is the case. You may be able to pattern your work so that there are changes of pace, personnel and tasks which will fulfil that need. If it is not possible at work, and if it is a need of yours, think of ways you can make your non-working time as kaleidoscopic as possible. If your need is being met even part of the time, your performance will improve.

Seeing a task through is the factor which makes energy flow in some cases. Cara Frances states:

> I like entrepreneurial excitement, creativity, following a job through and getting it done. I like commissioning something exciting and seeing it through to production.

And Janet King finds:

> I like delivery. I like getting things done, taking people with you in a collaborative way.

Perhaps, like Janet and Cara, you are a completer-finisher too. Notice how often, when and where in your work you have a chance to bring things to a resoundingly happy conclusion.

Job-satisfaction is elusive to define, but easy enough to feel. People know well enough whether they have it or not. If they do, it is a powerful motivating factor:

> What motivates me is a passion for understanding something. I have it at heart making sense of experience, making sense of the universe, and finding things out with the students, finding out together. (Paul Norton)

> I'm enjoying achieving changes in Equal Opportunities, and I'm enjoying being part of a team. I really do have a warm glow when I sit on the platform at the end of the year and the students are coming up and getting their diplomas. (Joan Yates)

> I'm a lazy introvert and so I like working in companies! It gives me people to talk to. Seriously, I am deeply interested in the work I do. It recalls and rekindles my imagination over and over again. (Julia Primera)

Leonard Rawlins also finds his genuine interest in and commitment to his company's values are key motivating factors:

> It's important for me that I really believe what the organization's about. However, good feedback is *easily* the number one motivator, number one by a long way.

Finding work we can truly be interested in and committed to is not always easy. Furthermore, career paths involve making choices that have long-term consequences, and our internal landscape may change while our career development moves inexorably along a direction we chose a number of years ago when our needs, expectations and values were different. Many managers perforce find themselves working in an industry or service or creative profession which they were attracted to in their twenties, but feel alienated from in their thirties and forties. Anyone in such a crisis (for although slow-burning, a crisis it certainly is) needs to look to both short-term and long-term planning to improve the situation. In the short term it is useful to analyse how, in your current job, you can find functions which *do* feel credible, worthwhile and satisfying. For example, you may be able to influence the corporate culture in some ways, or you may be able to set yourself personal targets which give shape and form to your time there. You may be able to form creative alliances with colleagues, or you may be able to make sure you use every opportunity in terms of training and development to broaden your own base while you are deciding what to do next.

In the long term, you do need to allow yourself time to consider whether you are going to make a radical career change or not. The macho manager pushes on through his or her emotional confusions towards the top of his or her company or profession even if internal signals of all kinds (depression, fatigue, illness, addiction, breakdown of relationships) are asking for a change. There are rewards for this and costs for this. The manager who is prepared to take his or her yin energies into account may respond differently. He or she may want to sit down and assess what is lacking in the present job, or what has changed inside themselves so as to create a disturbing imbalance between need and satisfaction of that need. The next question is what sort of change would fulfil the person's need for job satisfaction more, and how practical is that change within the person's life. It may be a matter of thinking through, maybe for weeks or even months, the implications of a major change in emphasis, direction or commitment at work. Can you afford to resign and retrain? Can you afford not to? Can you afford to change your attitude to your task at work or to your colleagues? Can you afford to change your goals in relation to your career? Can you afford not to? Allowing yourself to notice these questions and respond in your own time avoids the macho reaction. There are costs and rewards in this non-macho behaviour too. The choice is a matter for each person to take themselves, but the crucial thing is to be aware that it exists.

Motivating strategies

Thinking through what motivates us should help us to have a sense of how we can motivate others. It makes sense to try to create for them the kind of conditions which we find stimulating, encouraging and supportive ourselves. Some strategies emerge as key.

> I can be supportive and enthusiastic, and I can listen to people. (Julia Primera)

> I give plenty of good feedback. (Parminder Sharma)

Cara Frances enlarges on this by saying:

> I give lots of praise and lots of thanks. In this country [the UK] compared with the USA we are very poor at applauding. Achieving something is equated with being a goody-goody in some sense.

David Britton sees being generous with appropriate praise as a logical extension of his commitment to 'teams not stars'.

> I don't want a 'head' position so I'm happy to make sure other people feel important. I value their contribution and I listen to them. I ask them to do their own thing, communicate with me

about what they're doing, and give plenty of good feedback when they do well.

Good feedback has to be sincere to be valuable – a reflex 'well done' is little use to anyone, but a considered piece of praise makes a significant difference to almost anybody's day. When giving praise, or thanks, or positive feedback, we need to watch out for padding the positive message out with so much embarrassed verbiage that it is not clear (e.g. phrases like, 'I hope you don't mind me saying', 'sorry', 'you may think this is odd', and so forth.) The positive message should be short and clear. It should also be as specific as possible – it is more credible when someone says 'You did task x, interview y, report z, well', than if they say 'You're getting pretty good aren't you?' Positive feedback should be given as soon as possible after the successful event, so that the recipient of it gets the strongest connection between their successful behaviour and the pleasant sensation of being praised. (By contrast, negative feedback or criticism should be given as close to the next opportunity to get the behaviour *right* as possible, so that the sting of adrenaline that follows the criticism can be converted into energy to make a positive effort, and the information about *how* to change occurs very close to the *chance* to change.)

Our macho aspect may fear giving praise and positive feedback because it gives strength and power to others, weakening our hold on the situation. Our *yin* selves can conceive the matter differently, understanding that the more positive energy flows into a situation, the more everybody in that situation benefits. When a person's own self-esteem is flexible, grounded, and held with a light touch, there is no danger in the people around growing in self-respect as well.

It may be truly the case that in your organization it is dog eat dog, and that you have to be guarded and defended in every way in order to survive. Even if that is your reality, it is worth taking into account that praise can make extra energy available to subordinates and colleagues if that is what they, you, and the organization need at any particular time.

We have seen that it is important to managers to know *why*

they are doing what they are doing in order to get their energy and commitment properly behind it. It is equally important for the staff members to know too:

> I try to explain clearly what I want and why. I try to delegate properly. If I can't delegate a job I keep it to myself. 'Delegation' is a buzzword in my organization and a lot of people over-delegate with results that are not always good. (Sean McCann)

Specificity is important to Parminder Sharma too:

> I know how important it is to clarify things for people and help them with strategies. I try too to give them space to make mistakes. I don't always handle that too well. I think I'm too brittle.

The *yin* quality of intuition comes in here. Clear information is one element, but getting it received is the next.

> I can get onto other people's wavelengths and see their fears before they even speak them. (Derek Crispin)

Joan Yates speaks of:

> getting alongside people. That's the most important thing about motivating them: starting *with* them from *where they are now*.

This makes a particularly interesting contrast with the macho concept of 'leading from the front'. Perhaps we can consider a less macho alternative such as 'inspiring from next door'!

Getting onto somebody else's wavelength does not imply absorbing their neuroses or overlooking any sloppiness in their work. It simply means a degree of empathy which allows you to understand how they feel about whatever task faces them. It also allows you to work out how to be comprehensible, how to make maximum impact, how to sensitize yourself to what the positive 'turn-ons' and the negative 'turn-offs' are for them about their work and their personal inter-actions at work.

A 'radiant' (see p.102) example can provide high-calibre

motivation for subs and peers around it. A Detective Inspector speaks about a particular WPC on his force:

> I've seen men fall in behind Jackie because she is just so good at what she does. They've seen her in action, they know she's going to be doing the correct thing, so they just get in there with her and get the job done.

If your staff can see you, generally and with energy and conviction, getting the right thing done, it may be that that is all you need to do for them to 'fall in behind you' too. Simon Ayres feels that he motivates his staff partly at least by having 'apparently endless mental energy'. Because he can always find the intellectual and emotional capacity to see a problem through, they frequently find themselves to be capable of the same thing.

Good visioning is highly motivating to staff. Withholding the vision, the plan, in order to control it more completely, falls at the macho end of the spectrum. Both Chris Hargreaves and Janet King operate at the other end of that spectrum, where they can see staff responding well to sharing the plan.

> I really help people get going by communicating my belief that our goals are worthwhile, that these targets *are* achievable, we *can* overcome difficulties, we *can* be ambitious. (Chris Hargreaves)

> I prefer to be collaborative. I try to create openness, fairness, and clear accountability. I hate expediency and opportunism: so with my staff I try to give them a share of the action, so that they can do quality work and get quality outcomes. (Janet King)

A chance to define good results and then get good results is immensely heartening to the workers. The alternative of sloshing around in an organization not quite sure which drain your efforts are disappearing down, is really horrible.

How manipulative are you prepared to be in order to get your staff motivated? Michael Groves feels that the manipulative means are justified by the motivational ends:

> I have an ability to flirt with just about everybody, be they

women or men. For me it's part of getting to know people. If you ask people in the right way you can get them to do apparently impossible things. Use the stick and the feather duster, both judiciously, be patient, calm and encouraging, and give people confidence, but be rigorous too.

His insistence on high standards plus flexibility is shared by many managers, but his flair for flirting is present in fewer. It poses the question for those for whom it *is* an option, where, with whom, and how much to use it. Is it getting results from people under false pretences, or via an essentially corrupt interaction, or is it simply creative play with personal chemistry which enables people to flourish and fulfil their potential?

There is no easy answer to this one. Flirting could be coercive and destabilizing or it could be adult-to-adult, equal-to-equal, delightful improvization. In any particular case, your gut feel is probably your best sensor of what is going on. If you feel coerced, covertly dominated, or uneasy in any way, it is probably an interaction that is not useful to you. If you feel inventive and energized and *still in emotional equilibrium*, it may be a positive thing for you.

Leonard Rawlins has a strong view which not only rules out flirting, it rules out any hint of persuasive or coercive behaviour of any kind:

> I find the concept of motivation difficult. It feels manipulative to me. I wouldn't *want* to motivate anyone. I prefer to say, 'I will build a picture of the future, of what's going to happen, and if you enter into it, that's great.'

To many of us, Leonard's attitude would seem amazingly hands-off. Nevertheless, he presents a striking articulation of how to create and maintain energy and commitment in the workforce. Consider whether his way of work is a model which might be useful to you.

De-motivating factors

If we can get clear about what we feel de-motivated by, we can gain insights into what might de-motivate people generally, and thus some of the things we need to avoid with our staff.

Most intelligent people hate to be under-used.

> I am at my least motivated when I am not intellectually stimulated. I dislike it when I'm not extended, I dislike it when I'm scrabbling around for work to do.

The learning point here is simple but crucial. It shows that managers must be in touch with what their staff are doing, and if the work comes in in waves, they have to be prepared to find other genuinely constructive and developmental activities for them to get on with between waves. This means a non-macho acknowledgement of what is really going on rather than what we would like to be going on, or what would look good for the company or organization if it was going on. It means a non-macho preparedness to grow your staff and investigate their latent talents and abilities.

If it is you yourself who loathe the quiet times in a job that has its rushes and its low tides, do not wait for someone else to tell you what to do. At a time when you *do* feel positive, make some notes on background, technical, or developmental projects you could undertake during the next lull, and start to try to use those spaces in that positive way next time. Our macho model is that pressing ahead at full speed is the only potent, effective way to be. When we broaden out and take regard for our *yin* qualities we begin to appreciate the value of quiet growing times too.

Criticism can have a negative effect on our energy levels. Most people find criticism difficult, and some are frank enough to say exactly how much:

> I'm ridiculously over-sensitive to negative feedback. Recently I got one piece of negative feedback in my new job after eight months of glory. I was devastated! (Leonard Rawlins)

Ruefully he adds, 'I'm working on it.'

Both Derek Crispin and Phoebe Driscoll have approached this from the other way around, having become skilled and sensitive in *how* they make criticisms of their own staff members.

Derek says:

When it *is* necessary to criticize someone, I am careful to be tough on the issue and gentle on the person.

Phoebe points out:

I treat failure as a fact and not an emotion. I depersonalize it. I also remind people of their successes.

They have both reached the heart of what we need to be able to do to hear criticism clearly, learn from it, grow through it and not be destroyed by it.

The difference may look trivial, but psychologically it is all-important. If you criticize the *behaviour*, the person concerned can feel that they have an opportunity to change. If you criticize the *person*, they feel there is something intrinsically wrong with them, and are unlikely to feel as though they have the power to do anything about it. When you are the manager passing on negative feedback, *always* remember to criticize the behaviour and not the person. You may like to take note of Phoebe Driscoll's rebalancing idea too, of reminding people of their successes at the same time as you are asking them to take on board their failures. By separating the person and the issue, by lowering the emotional temperature surrounding criticism and dealing with mistakes and failures, you are emphatically enabling your member of staff to improve their performance next time.

What about being on the receiving end of criticism? Even if the person giving you the criticism does not have the skill to separate the person from the issues, you must take responsibility for doing this yourself. Listen to what the criticizer is saying. If they have personalized it, depersonalize it so that you are clear what the issue is. When you hear the issue, steady your breathing and consciously relax your muscles, and make a genuine assessment of whether it is correct or not. Avoid a brittle, macho, defensive response – it simply leads to the pantomime:

'Oh, no I didn't'
'Oh, yes you did'
'Oh no I couldn't'
'Oh yes you should have'
'Oh no I shouldn't'

– this will not get anybody anywhere. Realistically assess the criticism. If you do not agree, say so simply and assertively. If you do agree, say so simply, without excessive apology or rolling in the dirt. If you could obviously take specific, clear action to improve the situation, say so, again in a simple and assertive way.

The person who has criticized you may not take the opportunity to remind you of your successes. If they do not do so, take responsibility to do so for yourself. Connect yourself strongly with achievements you are genuinely proud of, times when you have worked well and felt competent and sure of yourself. Finally, although coping well with criticism gets easier with practice, there may still be a residue of unresolved emotional upset left when you have dealt with a critical reaction at work. Unless you have colleagues whom you deeply trust, work is probably not the place to deal with it. A trusted friend, a loved partner, or a 'speaking partner' – someone you have agreed to exchange support with – these are the people with whom you can appropriately share your left-over and unprocessed emotion. Those are the relationships within which we can express, explore, off-load, and get consolation and reassurance about this sort of upset. There is nothing wimpish about having needs like this, about acknowledging those needs to ourselves and others, and about seeking to get those needs met.

Poor information, poor procedures and poor follow-up de-motivate managers and staff alike. As we notice how negative and irritating these things are for us ourselves as managers, we must become more aware as the designers and providers of those things, how influential on morale they can be.

> I feel very demotivated when I rush to meet a deadline, and then the material I produce is not used. I am not inclined to make that kind of effort again for the same person. (Angela Winters)

When the goal posts move, you *must* tell the staff involved. They need to feel they had information on changes as soon as humanly possible, and they need to be given the respect and courtesy of an explanation if, as in this case, they were urged to rush a job and then see their results apparently wasted. If your boss moves the goal posts without warning you, you are perfectly entitled to express your reaction to the matter. If your work is wasted or rubbished because changes were not communicated down the line quickly and efficiently enough, again, it is useful to point this out to the senior tier. It is in their interests to know if they are pulling the plug on the workforce's commitment. Important information *can* be swiftly shared, and should be so.

Arcane procedures affect my motivation adversely.

When our efforts are undermined by factors beyond our control, we do feel we are banging our heads against a brick wall.

– Janet King and Chris Hargreaves respectively voice their complaints about bad systems.

When you are in a position to design or influence the design of systems and procedures, *always* look to streamlining and slimming down. Also, *always* ask yourself basic questions about what the system is supposed to *do*. Most organizations more than five years old have a considerable archaeology of systems designed for function (a), adapted for function (c), (d) and (e), and now used for (y) and (z) since (a) is no longer done, the law has changed on (d), and (e) is carried out by a subsidiary branch in another city. Furthermore, the person who takes care of function (c) is on very bad terms with the branch manager who takes care of (e) and is worried that he is trying to empire-build: so he tends to complicate matters around (e) anyway. You get the picture. You have *worked* in the picture! Thus, whenever you reorganize procedures and systems go back to absolute first principles about what needs doing, what is needed to do it, who needs to check it, and who needs to know.

'Brick walls' exist in most of our workplaces. They may be intensely frustrating commercially, they may be tragic socially, depending on the nature of our work. We do need to take care of changing the culture so that brick walls can be dismantled. This is fundamental to unblocking organization. We also need to take care of ourselves and our staff while the brick walls do still exist. As managers we have to give committed and realistic support to staff who feel they are hitting a brick wall. We have to give them the inspiration to believe it is still worth while carrying on. We have to create a faith in them that we are working to knock the brick wall down. We have to be able to pull the team together and keep morale viable. For our own selves we may need to think of getting the emotional needs created by this situation met elsewhere. A trusted friend, a loving partner, or a 'speaking partner', can allow us the space to express the doubts, frustrations and pain of colliding with a 'brick wall', console us and encourage us to evolve solutions. Needing kindness and attention when there are serious problems like this at work is not a weakness. Conversely, noticing the need, respecting it and seeking to have it met, is an example of flexible strength.

Every job has passages which simply do not suit:

> I'm turned off by things that are not of the mind. I can't get any energy up for working for long-term political change. I'm very hands-on, and abstract things alienate me. (Simon Ayres)

> I don't like working with the same people all the time. I don't like too much detail and I don't like repetition of tasks. (Neil Glover)

You can easily pick out the strands of your own job that you dislike. Do not let them take on a mythological value. Keep them in their place by being organized and effective, getting them done in contained bits of time, and not allowing doing them or the dread of doing them spoil the parts of your job that you do enjoy. Use your flexible imagination to view your job as one with lights and shadows in it, as an entirely natural thing. Use the light touch of your awareness to notice if the non-enjoyable elements of the job begin to outweigh the enjoyable ones and, if so, to respond in whatever way is practical and realistic as well as being self-respecting and self-valuing.

Lastly, in this section which focuses on factors which might de-motivate us ourselves, do notice with humour and self-respect any qualities in your own personality which might make it difficult for you to be motivated.

I don't like being told what to do by anybody else. Ever. (Julia Primera)

I've come to the conclusion that I am fundamentally un-manageable. I don't trust anybody else's intentions or judgement either. (Sean McCann)

If that is how you are, you are going to have a hard time picking up any motivational kilowatts from anybody else at all: in other words, you will have to do it all yourself, as well as handling yourself so that your resentment of being directed by someone else does not show, until you are in the driving seat of the operation yourself. In fact there is nothing to worry about unless you become blocked by this. It is simply a matter of applying the non-macho, or yin principles of fluency, flexibility, acceptance and development, to qualities which are strong and intrinsic to you, and not immediately apparently conducive to professional success. One has to think the matter through, and act with self-knowledge and equilibrium.

Turning off the workers

We all turn the staff off sometimes. Recognizing these disasters is not an invitation to despair: it is, rather, the first step in putting things right. It may be helpful to share confessions of many managers who *know* they have, from time to time, turned their workers off.

I'm too critical, sometimes people meet with a crushing response with me. And another thing, when I'm really uncomfortable, I withdraw and become cold. People suddenly feel hurt and punished. I'm aware of what I'm doing, but not of how terrible it's making everyone else feel. (Simon Ayres)

I criticise too much – don't give enough strokes. I don't always know precisely what's happening for my staff, and I don't always look after them as much as they would like. (Siobhan Boyle)

Julia Primera is aware that she is sometimes intolerant, and sometimes a truly terrible delegator:

> I want people to get things right, but I'm afraid that by 'right', I mean *my* way. I am intolerant when other people screw up and set ridiculously high standards. My husband pointed out that when I went away for two days I left more notes for the nanny than he does when he leaves his multi-national chemical plant to go away to the USA for two weeks.

David Britton understands that interpersonal skills are not his strongest suit:

> I have a miserable face. I never say 'good morning' to anyone. My body language is terribly off-putting, and when I am busy I am over-brisk.

Neil Glover knows that he assumes an off-putting artificial persona from time to time:

> When I feel defensive I start to come over a bit stridently as 'an expert'.

Chris Hargreaves feels that on occasion he is pedestrian in the extreme:

> There are times when I am just going through the routine, not encouraging anyone or inspiring anyone at all.

Her deep commitment to sharing does not always shape Joan Yates' behaviour.

> I can be totally autocratic, and make decisions and expedite business very abruptly. I forget to tell people things and they feel left out and put down.

> I'm very demanding [says Janet King]. Sometimes it's difficult for people to live up to my expectations. I'm over-confident at times, think very quickly, and jump in too quickly.

Paul Norton can see that he 'turns off the workers' at times because of particular fears of his own.

I find it hard to make mistakes in public. I lack confidence in my own organizational abilities, and so face all that with enormous reluctance. I'm a back-seat driver when it comes to initiatives and tend to let the agenda be set by other people.

Parminder Sharma reflects:

I may make other people feel unwanted. Sometimes I dump stuff on them.

And Sean McCann knows that:

I do take people for granted. Sometimes I am insufficiently decisive.

Any or all of those might ring bells for you. You can balance the angst of recognizing your own deficiencies with the knowledge that at least one other person is just as bad! The failures in motivating staff tend to spring from overdoing macho actions and reactions – such as being over-confident, loud, and autocratic, or from falling into the opposite, passive mode, i.e. being bored and flat, or unable to take initiatives. We need to notice where we do fail to motivate our staff, and then to notice that everyone is allowed to make mistakes, have lapses, have room for improvement. We cannot alter temperamental tendencies immediately by an act of will, but we can, with the greatest of self-respect, become aware of where we do go wrong, and begin to make small specific changes for improvement.

The good-enough motivator

The basics of good staff motivation, taking a broad and flexible view which incorporates the *yin* and the *yang*, the ebb and the flow, the dark and the light, moves away from the military or macho model.

The essentials are to:

- Inspire – by vision and example.

- Instruct – ensure everyone has the skills and information they need.

- Get the rhythm right – balance urgency with calm times, seriousness with humour.

- Set the boundaries – set high standards of integrity and practice for yourself and for others.

- Stand back – do not breathe down anybody's neck. Remember credit where credit is due.

Conflict resolution

You can sort conflicts out by overwhelming or outwitting your opponent. There are times when that will be necessary. There are also times when you may like to consider the alternative approach of conflict resolution where you look for win-win solutions. No one is overpowered, no one is out-manoeuvred, and both parties emerge with a satisfactory compromise and an ability to move forwards. This outcome can be arrived at by means of:

- assertive communication
- negotiation with a fall-back position
- agreed resolution

Assertive communication

Before the 1980s we had a rather hazy concept of what being a powerful negotiator was all about. It was to do with flair and charisma, and was the preserve mostly of men, mostly between the ages of twenty-five and forty-five and mostly white. You either 'had it' or you did not. It was an ability to cope in the cut and thrust developed, largely, by going to a certain kind of school, being groomed through a certain kind of career, and being very familiar with the private languages and coded behaviours of their particular field.

This had the effect of excluding women, black people, the disabled, and any other group that could not penetrate and assimilate these pathways, codes and languages.

The assertiveness movement, inaugurated in the UK by Anne

Dickson in the early 1980s, was a revelation. It provided a pragmatic, common-sense communication technique, which could hold its own in the most excluding and hostile environment. It also posited an alternative way of doing business. Most importantly of all, it could be learned. You did not have to have it to the manner born.

Anyone could learn to use it and so transact their business with dignity and composure and without being intimidated. It is an indispensable skill for the manager who wants to be a good leader with an ability to resolve conflicts without behaving in a macho way.

Briefly, assertiveness is based on:

- recognizing four different types of behaviour that arise during a conflict
- having a calm sense of self-esteem
- communicating clearly and concisely
- sticking to your point without getting distracted or upset

Four types of behaviour

When tense, threatened, or challenged, we tend to respond in one of the following ways:

directly aggressive:	i.e.	shouting, accusing, table-thumping, over-angry
indirectly aggressive:	i.e.	sarcastic manipulative, creating uncomfortable atmospheres, being two-faced and inconsistent
passive:	i.e.	victim-like, martyrish, hopeless, whining
assertive:	i.e.	respectful of self and others, level, steady, taking responsibility for self, knowing when to persist and when to let go

With practice we can quickly recognize these types of behaviour both in ourselves and others. We can make a decision to move more often into the assertive mode and less often into the others. In particular we can practise taking an assertive stance when under a great deal of pressure, and when dealing with an interlocutor who is in one of the other modes.

A calm self-esteem

Appropriate self-esteem has been a recurrent theme throughout this book. The typical macho tendency is to be either inappropriately high or inappropriately despairing about our abilities. Again, with practice, we can be clear about and accept both our strengths and our weaknesses. This makes us very much less tense, very much less dependent on anybody else's good opinion. Aggressive attacks have less effect, and so facilitating solutions to conflict is much easier.

Clear concise communication

A core phrase which expresses your point is an invaluable part of assertiveness technique. Avoid unnecessary padding ('I'm sorry', 'could you possibly', 'this may sound stupid but').

Own strong feelings, do not *dump* them, by making 'I' statements:

- 'I feel angry about that'
  NOT
  'You're making me angry'

- 'I believe that was a mistake'
  NOT
  'You got it wrong'

- 'I think this is urgent'
  NOT
  'Hurry up'

Sticking to your point

Once you have your core phrase, which expresses what you need to say in a given situation, you can stick to it in a light-touch and

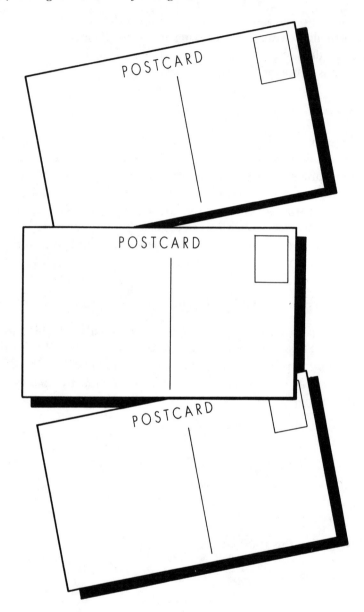

flexible way by reacting assertively to aggressive, indirectly aggressive, or passive reactions which aim to undermine you. Simply show you've heard what the other person said, then repeat your core phrase.

'I realize you feel very angry about x, but we still need to sort out y.'

'I understand that you want to hurry this decision through, but we must establish a b and c first.'

'I know you feel very upset by X's behaviour. Do let us get task y out of the way and then we can address the matter.'

Here are three postcards. You can send one each to a person in your working life to whom you need to say something. By fitting the message onto the postcard you will have to distill it into a clear core phrase. Think over what it would be like to be as clear and assertive with this person. Simple though it is, this is a very good exercise for seeing how to unstick relationships which are bogged down at work. You might or might not actually say the core phrase on the postcard but you will clear your head about what is going on and what needs to happen.

Have one more postcard if you want. On it, write the message that you need to give yourself.

Negotiating with a fall-back position

Before you enter into any negotiations for resolving conflict, work out your fall-back position. It is like attending an auction – you need to know in advance what your top bid will be. Only in the most exceptional circumstances do you compromise on it. If you have advance notice of a situation where you will have to negotiate, you have time to think through your fall-back. If a situation blows up suddenly, make it part of your assertive self-discipline to work out your fall-back position instantly. In that case it will have to be an intuitive or gut-feel choice; but it is important because it gives immediate shape and boundaries to your reactions, and the people dealing with you will sense that you are firm and strong without being brittle.

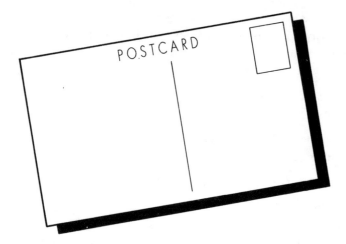

An agreed solution

If you are using assertiveness to resolve a conflict between two staff members, or a conflict amongst a whole team or committee, or a conflict between a staff member and yourself, you are looking for a win–win solution from which all parties will walk away with dignity.

- *Empathize* with all parties. Make sure they have their say, and that they know you have heard properly. Do not, however, get sucked into their emotions. Check that all parties have listened carefully to each other. Set boundaries so that nobody rants, raves, or rambles.

- *Express* your own point of view, without padding, without being intimidating or manipulative. Make sure they have heard and understood you.

- *Evolve* a solution that has something positive in it for everybody. Do not be tokenist about it. It must have a genuine plus point for everybody.

- *Trade* within the limits of your fall-back position. Controlled give-and-take will benefit everyone, but make sure nobody gets steamrollered at this point.

- *Affirm* everybody's agreement before drawing to a close. Do not force a champagne celebration on people unless they are genuinely delighted by the outcome, but try to get all parties to voice (literally, out loud) their positive agreement with the solution you have all evolved. This makes an important symbolic commitment on their part.

Using conflict resolution in this way enhances the health both of the organization – it gets a chance to implement new ideas and grow – and its members, who truly know they will be heard and responded to. It is also very much less costly in terms of energy to the manager who has to facilitate the conflict – rather than trying to carry it off by force of personality there is a positive structure to use.

7. And one more thing

We have now unravelled, knitted back up, analysed, spread out, examined, and prowled around all kinds of aspects of managerial behaviour, and at every stage said to ourselves – is it effective to be macho here? What would happen if we were not? What would being non-macho in this context involve? and what are the checks and balances? We have shared the thoughts and experiences of many managers faced with the same questions, and there have been some surprises. We have looked at times when it seemed that being macho was the only solution, and times when avoiding it seems to open out vistas of new possibilities.

Let us give ourselves, and indeed the managers we have worked with all this time, the opportunity to say 'one more thing' about the whole issue.

TRIGGER ELEVEN:

Now that you have thought about taking the macho out of management, is there one point or one discovery you would like to take time to notice now?

Make a note of what comes into your mind here. Do not censor it or try to construct it as worthy or mature or deep – whatever has risen to the top of your consciousness is what you need to notice now.

In expressing their 'one more thing', the managers who contributed to this book became quite epigrammatic, and their epigrams then suggest links with the Taoist thinking which is the door through which we came in. Taoist philosophers are no horizon-gazing withdrawn theorists – they are strategists, survivors and warriors. They are not only useful to members of current society who want to be contemplative, they are useful to those of us who need to be intensely pragmatic and active too. Remember that the favourite book of the (anti)-hero of the movie *Wall Street* was Sun Tzu's *The Art of War* (now available with the more intelligently translated title *The Art of Strategy* in a version by R. L. Wing). Our need to do several things at once and to do them all well, and our need to prevail and succeed effectively in *all* our roles, in *all* our multiple commitments, is particularly susceptible in illumination by Taoist text. Being able to respond with all our senses at once – gut-feel and intellect, defence-awareness and initiative-awareness, short-term advantage and long-term gain, is the long study of these monks and warriors ancient and modern. Their theory and practice (because they would never give any credence to one without the other) resonate well with our longing for the patterning of success into our lives without the wrecking of our health, our loving relationships, or our sense of collegiateness with team and colleagues.

Let us look at a final thought from some of our managers, and link it in, where appropriate, with some Taoist thought. Notice when and where these ideas are surprising and contentious to you, and when and where, although you might not have articulated them before, they are strangely familiar.

Firstly, Parminder Sharma comes up with an apposite description of how the non-macho manager shares tasks: 'Delegate, but don't abdicate'. She perceives here the essential ingredient of letting the task go in a generous and constructive way, but continuing a link of responsibility. One envisages immediately a kind of sliding scale where, the more difficult or risky the job, the greater the 'parental' and nurturing support of the delegating manager, and their commitment to remain as a resource and source of advice being firm; but equally, if the task is not demanding or complicated, a sense of almost complete letting-go, with only a slender thread still linking the two. Unnecessary checking-up and nagging disappears in this epigrammatic vision, but a flexible linkage of responsibility *is* there. 'Abdication' is a brilliant word for what happens when, under the mask of delegation, which is always a right-on thing to be doing (see Sean McCann's comment: 'it's a buzzword in my organization' p.110), the manager simply dumps. What easier and more convenient way to get rid of tasks that are so mind-numbingly boring we never want to even think about them again, or so awkward (acerbic clients, elusive suppliers, legal/technical hassles), that the time they take on the real clock is three times the time they ought to take on paper so one does not even want to start them and start the inexorable meter ticking – what easier way to dispense with these unpleasant tasks than to abdicate them on to juniors, preferably never giving them another thought? We have all done it at one time or another. Well, indeed part of the function of delegation is to give the more mature, experienced minds in a company or organization more space and time to talk to the more difficult and complex tasks, but wholesale dumping like this is definitely macho and will cause problems later with the team in terms of resentment, lost loyalty and bad role-modelling. Preserving the link, skilfully making it clear that you remain ultimately responsible but do not wish actively to take up the reins of that responsibility except in an emergency, is a more effective use of strength. Be aware of and use this concept the other way around too. You may feel your boss, on occasion, abdicates to you. You may have an uncomfortable sense of having all the responsibility with none of the power. If so, acknowledge to yourself that the position is uncomfortable and untenable, and try some assertive communication to point the situation out. It will probably be useful to use Parminder's formulation in your own mind but the words would be too provocative to give to your boss as an opening statement. (They would be highly satisfactory in the event of a showdown!). Try an 'I' statement stating your discomfort, e.g.

I feel very isolated dealing with this case.

and a constructive suggestion:

Until it is resolved I feel I need five minutes or so to discuss it with you once a week.

with a fall-back position clear in your own mind: e.g. if he/she will not agree to a regular discussion, put a memo on progress in the file once a week and insist on a brief review meeting once a month.

Sun Tzu analysed the art of strategy exhaustively. He thought long and hard about how to delegate in such a way as to get other people to do what you want them to:

Commands that are straightforward
Will enlighten others and result in their obedience.

Commands that are not straightforward
Will not enlighten others or bring their obedience.

Those who can set forth commands with absolute credibility can
bring the numerous together in success.

(Sun Tzu, *The Art of Strategy* 36 Aquarian, 1989)

Leonard Rawlins says:

> If there is one thing that characterizes any concept of a good
> leader now, it is that there has to be openness *and* a structure. I
> have come across so many people who are really terrible
> leaders because they try to be *just* open and collaborative. You
> *must* make a framework and brief people clearly as well.

In a sense, he is describing the mess that happens when someone,
stereotypically in an 'enlightened' arts-based or commitments-
based organization (charity, voluntary organization, educational
or medical institution) takes up a managerial role absolutely
determined to be democratic, approachable and non-macho.

Their open-door, listening and flexible approach is admirable
as far as it goes, but it is finally ineffective. Setting the boundaries,
both in systems, structures and policies, is essential in allowing
creativity genuinely to happen. Failing to set those boundaries is a
mistake we make when we are putting a high priority on
showing how much we value other people's input, how respon-
sive we can be to news and suggestions, and how little
hierarchical status means to us. Moving too far in that direction
can unbalance the whole organization and paradoxically make
the input, the news and suggestions of the junior person very
much less likely to be effectively used. Only when the systems
and structures are organized, contained and integrated, can
collaborative development be held in place and allowed to grow.
It is important to be a leader, and not just everybody's friend.

Openness has been a kind of watchword throughout this book:
inform, inform, inform – do not hold back, do not hold out on
anybody. However, Leonard's insight about there being leaders

who fail because they are too open gives us the clue that the right level of containment is important too. Sometimes the background, information and opinion which we pass onto people is loading which they do not need. Sometimes we can respect our own tiredness, or need for privacy, or even irritability, and *not* share everything which is theoretically shareable. Dainin Karigin expresses this beautifully.

> If somebody asks you about doctrines, sometimes you can discuss them, but sometimes you can say you are busy.

(Dainin Karigin, *Returning to Silence*, Shambhala, 1988)

What a relief, what a revelation, what a joy! Anyone who, because they are in possession of a particular skill or technique or ideology, has felt compelled to explain it fully to anyone who ever asks a question, will be delighted by this thought. You are allowed not to sometimes. You are allowed not to from time to time simply because you *do not feel like it*. It is the same point that tells us that included within assertiveness technique is the right, whenever you wish, *not* to be assertive; and it is the same point which is symbolized by the dark half of the yin-yang symbol containing a dot or seed of light, and the light half of the yin/yang symbol containing a dot or seed of darkness.

Equal Opportunities matters featured in the 'one more thing' added by some of the managers we spoke with. Michael Groves says:

> The thing which comes into my mind is that I prefer my management team not to be male dominated. There are a number of reasons for this: one is that it reduces or even removes the pornography from around you. If there are obscene discussions going on, at least you have two points of view on it. Actually archaeologists tend to have a vulgar sense of humour, possibly because within the subject everything within mankind [sic] is acceptable.
>
> On the ideological side, I once had a very committed Christian working alongside a very committed Muslim. I did, in the end, have to tell them to discuss religion in their own time.

Michael essentially has an optimistic view of Equal Opportunities development, where things *are* gradually getting better,
and barriers *are* coming down. Maybe fields of endeavour such as
archaeology really do create an intellectual open-mindedness
which helps to facilitate the process of change in the here and
now. Angela Winters is struck by how much in gender terms the
men in her industry still need protecting from talented women,
and – what really depresses her – that the women still take it upon
themselves to do the protecting:

> I was involved in a project with a very senior female colleague
> and four other senior and very expert women. The final
> meeting involved presenting the project to the top brass: it
> could have been a bit of a showdown. The man with all the
> say, the major top man, was not able to cope with this array of
> strong women, and what we had to do was to remove the four
> women of the team from the meeting, so that he was not
> confronted with so many women all at once.
>
> I began to understand why it was necessary because he was
> an insecure person and seemed jumpy: he was antagonistic and
> not constructive. His idea of negotiation was to knock down
> and condemn ideas. With more women present it would have
> been even more difficult.
>
> I wish we had not done things that way and it did not feel a
> positive conclusion, but it was the final hurdle and if we had
> not compromised the whole project might have crashed.
>
> I found it a very salutary experience. I was furious, but I did
> understand that on that occasion it was the only way. Having
> said that, I hope I never experience anything like that again. A
> woman with these qualities of insecurity would never have
> arrived at a senior post like that man.

Predicaments like these are, unfortunately, fairly common,
where the group discriminated *against* ends up nursing the group
who are doing the discriminating while they face up to a more
egalitarian future. The only way of surviving this is to make a
decision each time on the relative importance of the survival of
the project and the furthering of Equal Opportunities, and to

decide when you are quite clear that you are not going to do anybody else's emotional housework for them.

Julia Primera sees a rising star of leadership qualities among a great many women, nominating Glenys Kinnock and Hilary Clinton (President of the Mother's Union) among them. The latter she celebrates as 'able to visit orphans in the Himalayas and bake cakes in a vicarage', and says, 'Women are the unsung heroes of our society.'

We should not underestimate the upheaval to us all in trying to create a more fair and equitable workplace. We should not underestimate the ugliness of discrimination and the waste of resources engendered by *not* singing our heroes. We can from time to time pause from anger, campaigning, despair, or trying to shift things, to home in on some of the very quiet and grounded thoughts of the philosophers:

> . . . hatred can never put an end to hatred; love alone can. This is an unalterable law. People forget that their lives will end soon. For those who remember, quarrels come to an end.

(*Dhammapada* 1:5,6)

This is not to trivialize oppression or show disrespect for the value of action. It is, however, to say that, however desperate the issues, life is short. It offers the Buddhist affirmation that love, in the end, is the only force which can overcome everything else.

Cara Frances looks on the necessity of being circumspect – that you never know when fate will tip the balance of your relationship with people, so you should behave well in all circumstances:

> I think you must take a very professional approach with everyone. They may be junior to you now, but they may be ahead of you in a few years.

This salutary thought makes sense in the face of the general instability of most industries in the nineties and the fact that, for example, taking time out for further training or for a parental break may put you out of sync with your former peers. There is no need to crawl, but a light and dignified assertiveness with everyone at all times can save you from an embarrassing wrench if your relative seniorities suddenly change. Parminder has a further thought on emotionally safe practice. She is speaking both of herself as a non-macho manager, and of what she would like from her own boss:

> I do think a manager who is not concerned with being macho can afford to create a safe environment for you to take risks in. They can guide you through the treacherous waters.

Respecting everyone in the organizational culture, whether you like them or not (and indeed, finding out just how well you can work with people you do not 'like' is one of the unexpected pleasures of moving away from macho defensiveness), and nurturing everyone in the organizational culture likewise, may be a shift for you but it can be a profoundly beneficial one. It takes on board the Taoist holistic view of the universe.

> Implicit in Western science is the notion that nature exists to be plundered.
>   Taoism and eastern philosophies without exception take the view that such plundering affects the whole, that man is not separate from nature when he does things to it, extracts things from it. On the contrary, he is an integral part of nature, and everything he does, he does to himself.

(Page, *The Power of Ch'i*, Aquarian, 1988)

It has never been more urgent for the survival of the planet that we reflect on this. It applies to all our social units too – our families, our companies, our cities and our states. Take time to absorb this thought.

Various points arose in people's minds about resolving the paradox of being non-macho but visualizing the leading roles in an organization in the 'pedestal position'. Phoebe Driscoll gives some useful clues as to how to reorganize our reactions:

> Giving someone a title doesn't necessarily give them the attributes to fulfil it. Senior people are often brittle in order to defend their sense of 'automatic rightness'. When you are dealing with people senior to yourself, think to yourself 'Would I employ this person?' This will help you see through their mystique to their real qualities.

This is a helpful and practical suggestion. Once you start to do it, you get some interesting results!

Neil Glover has an analysis which is equally thought-provoking:

> The key roles are not always the *top* roles. Ask yourself, if person A or person B is absent, how long is it before you notice? This gives you some idea how important they really are.

Apply this criterion to different personnel in your organization. It may give you some interesting insights into who the cornerstones of the operation really are. Valuing people according to their real contribution rather than their official title is a way of beginning to dismantle the macho mystique which may hover around the *names* of the top jobs. Siobhan Boyle's view is informed by her passionate concern with the growth of women's participation in leadership roles.

> Pyramidic managerial structures are alien to women. There should be flatter organizations with more cross-sharing, and value given for co-operative working in both funding and standing.

Siobhan has expended enormous energy in this field, but at the moment feels positive change seems a long way away:

> I don't know what the answers are. Women will never make it except as quasi-males at the moment. I have struggled with this long and hard. I want to be the initiator in my team, but I *don't* want to be the superior.

There is a resonance between the conception of 'leader' or 'instructor' in the oriental arts and Siobhan's longing to be an initiator but not a superior. Although instructors in yoga and martial arts are respected and implicitly trusted and obeyed, their extra experience is treated as a fact, not a virtue. Senior teachers of yoga are called 'guru'. The two syllables of 'guru' simply mean 'taker-away of darkness' – so a guru is someone who gets rid of the darkness of not-knowing and not-understanding.

C. W. Nichol explains the derivation of the word 'sensei' – the name for the instructor in the Japanese fighting arts:

> The Japanese character 'seu' means 'ahead' or 'before'. The character 'sei' has the essence of many meanings – 'life', 'birth', 'pure', 'genuine', 'raw'. If the two words are put together they form the word 'sensei', which is poorly translated as 'teacher'.
>
> (C. W. Nicol, *Moving Zen: Karate as a Way to Gentleness*, Crompton, 1981)

It seemed useful to some people to point out that a calm, generous and non-macho manager has to be prepared to be isolated from time to time. He or she will sometimes be unpopular, or taking a line which in spite of their best endeavours nobody understands, or defending policy when staff wish they could persuade them to alter it. Being able to cope with that aloneness is a valuable strength.

> To be a manager who avoids the macho traps, you mustn't want to be liked by everyone. You do get a lot of admiration sometimes, but you've got to be able to cope without it. Respect for work done is the essential. I think it is potentially lonely. I can think of the example of one of our professors who was desperate for allies, and so made friends with the youngest people on the staff because they were the most approachable. Politically it was disastrous. The others felt left out, factions formed. (Paul Norton)

David Britton feels the same, and says simply: 'It is sometimes lonely.'

Those of us who have worked in offices or institutions beyond the honeymoon period of the new team and the new enterprise know how extraordinarily lonely it sometimes is, even in a crowded office, even with clients coming in and out all day, even in the middle of a buzz of activity. If you have something on your mind, or a difficult line to hold, you can feel very alone all the same. The Dhammapada tells us what to do in a typically straightforward simple way.

> If you find no one to support you on the spiritual path, walk alone.
>
> (*Dhammapada* 1:5,6)

Loneliness cycles back to togetherness or belonging in the end; it is a question of peaceful waiting.

Let us consider a point made by Lieh-Tzu, a Chinese philosopher of the fifth century BC.

> In the world there is a Way by which one will always conquer and there is a Way by which one will never conquer. The former is called Weakness and the latter is called Strength. The two are easy to recognise, but still men do not recognise them.
>
> (Lieh-Tzu, trans. A. C. Graham, *The Yellow Emperor*)

You may need to read this once or twice, since the opposition is set up in the opposite way to that which you might expect. The meaning is that modesty and fluidity will triumph over aggression and violence. It does not mean compromising and being weak in the sense of undefined and feeble, but having a paradoxical power by not forcing things.

Simon Ayres finds this.

> I'm learning to lead from behind. It's taking a huge shift to deal with the anxiety caused by standing back – but I'm doing it.

Taking the same line, we will leave the last comment to David Britton who runs his complex international operation not by cracking the whip, not by making a lot of noise and performance about being the big chief, but by taking a non-macho, simple and vigorous line.

> With commonsense, honesty, and goodwill, there is *nothing* that cannot be achieved.

Final checklist

I hope this book has shaken up, revitalized and changed your thinking about the necessities of management in the real world, and the choices you might make about it. To gather your thoughts together and formulate your action planning, use this checklist.

- What was the most surprising thing you came across while reading and reacting to this book?

- What was the most worrying thing you came across?

- What was the most hopeful or inspiring fact or idea you came across?

- What insights have arisen for you about your own practice?

- What insights have arisen for you about the way things are done in your organization?

- What action plans would you like to make? This table may be helpful:

	Issue	Action Plan	When?	With What Support?
1				
2				
3				
4				
5				

(Action planning always works better when you work out the time-frame it would be useful to achieve it in, and what kind of support may be helpful in your achieving it.)

I hope that the reviewing, re-thinking, and application of fresh thinking to your way of doing your particular job make a positive difference – and broaden out all the perspectives and options so that for you, taking the macho out of management becomes a real and productive possibility.

Further Reading

Charles Handy, *Gods of Management: The Changing Work of Organizations*. Business Books 1991

John Heider, *The Tao of Leadership*. Wildwood House 1986

Vanessa Helps, *Negotiating: Everybody Wins*. BBC 1992

Sam Keen, *Fire in the Belly: On Being a Man*. Piatkus 1992

Peter Middleton, *The Inward Gaze: Masculinity and Subjectivity in Modern Culture*. Routledge 1992

Paddy O'Brien, *Positive Management: Assertiveness for Managers*. Brealey Publishing 1992

Naomi Wolf, *The Beauty Myth: How Images of Beauty are Used Against Women*. Vintage 1991

Index